Puchka
In The
Polder

Shayonti Chatterji
Reshmi Nashier
Satyakirty Akhouri

notionpress
.com

INDIA · SINGAPORE · MALAYSIA

ISBN
Paperback 979-8-89906-993-2
Hardcase 979-8-89961-838-3

CONTENTS

PRAISE FOR THE BOOK

Some books entertain, some inform, and then there are those rare ones that quietly settle into your soul this is one of them. This collection of deeply personal and evocative stories is a testament to the lives of three women who carry two worlds within them: the homeland they left behind and the one they now call home.

Threaded with themes of identity, belonging, love, and loss, these stories take you through the richness of lived experience be it the quiet heartbreak of seeing your mother's wrinkles in your own reflection, the comfort of childhood meals cooked by loving hands, the ache of cultural displacement, or the realization that time, love, and family slip through our fingers faster than we can hold them

This is not just a book it is a mirror, a time capsule, a warm embrace. A must-read for anyone who has ever loved, longed, or found themselves standing at the crossroads of who they were and who they are becoming.

Shaurya Gahlawat,
Psychologist & Writer

Puchka in Polder felt like tuning into an episode of Desi Junction a heartfelt connection to home, aapke watan se rishta. Just like our weekly radio show, these stories are fun, engaging, and steeped in nostalgia, taking you on a journey through time, food, aging, and life's musings.

Each anecdote peels back layers of memory, much like an old song or a familiar aroma that instantly transports you to another time. The bilingual storytelling seamlessly blending English with Hindi transliterations echoes how many of us think, feel, and reminisce, making it all the more relatable.

Puchka in Polder is a slice of life, a reminder that no matter where we go, the echoes of our roots stay with us. Just as Desi Junction bridges continents through music and memories, this book builds a bridge through words bringing warmth, humor, and a deep sense of belonging.

Jassi Parmar,
CEO Desi Junction

Puchka in the Polder- First of all the title made me smile as Puchka or pani puri is my mother's most favourite snack amongst the many amazing snacks of India. This book gives you insight in the journey of Indian womanhood. Also, the book reveals the way the writers become members of the Dutch community and culture but still long for their roots back home.

It is about linking to your roots, sharing your sense of belonging and how these craving colours daily live. It is an inspiration. Sharing insights between generations and between cultures make us a stronger community worldwide. It makes us empowered and more connected to our roots and to our way of becoming and belonging in the Netherlands.

Artie Ramsodit
Coach, mentor, politician (Dutch Senator)

The book will be an inspiration to young and old. It provides a cultural outside in look by women who have been stepping out of their cultural comfort zones into another one, looking therefore at life's events and challenges through a different lens, providing inspiration, resilience and keeping the respect and celebrating the beauty of their cultural heritage within their new context.

Helene van der Roest
Board of Directors,
ESG and Development Advisor

The authors skilfully convey their personal experiences of growing up in an India that is still waking up to her strengths. They poignantly illustrate the harsh realities that women across the country have faced, including social injustice, systemic inequality, and cultural expectations, as well as the ongoing struggles they continue to endure. Each narrative serves as a testament to the resilience, courage, and unwavering strength of these women.

True stories of courage, faith & hope, the stories touch you with their sheer honesty.

Kamna Hazrati
Founder - AndPurpose

Reading "Puchka in the Polder" felt like an intimate conversation with friends who deeply understand the nuanced challenges of living between cultures, where values collide and perspectives shift in subtle yet profound ways. Like the authors, I live between two lenses: one shaped by the country I left behind years ago, and another continually adjusted to embrace my adopted Dutch home. The magic of this collection is how effortlessly it speaks to anyone who has ever stood between two worlds, neither fully here nor there, yet finding beauty and wisdom precisely in that delicate balance. Over time, this delicate harmony deepens, evolving as we age through layers of introspection, acceptance, and a richer understanding of our complex identities. Beyond these reflections, what resonated deeply was the tender nostalgia for people and meals left behind, those spontaneous moments with loved ones, shared around tables filled with comfort food from home. An honest, heartfelt, and universally resonant exploration. Truly special.

Chris Parker,
Executive, Coach, Author

PREFACE

What you are holding in your hands is a book born from passion, shaped by curiosity, and woven from the lived experiences of three women of Indian origin who, over the past two decades, have made Amstelveen, Netherlands, their home. It grew organically, much like most memoirs, through shared moments, deep reflections, and a desire to capture the essence of life between two worlds.

Much like the Dutch polders, land reclaimed through hard work, this book reclaims voices and emotions often lost in time. And just like a *puchka*, bursting with unexpected flavours, it holds nostalgia, raw emotions, and the bittersweet reality of straddling two worlds. Some stories will make you smile, others may bring a lump to your throat, but all will remind you of life's unpredictability, just like that extra-spicy puchka you didn't see coming!

Welcome to *Puchka in the Polder*

The Journey Begins . . .

It all started with a book club, a way to reconnect with Hindi literature, a language familiar yet slipping away under the dominance of English. Each member had a different relationship with Hindi, one was fluent but hadn't truly explored its literary depths, another could read the script but wasn't well-versed in its richness, and the third had a natural command over it. But what united them was a love for books, both classic and contemporary.

What began as a reading circle soon became something much more- a journey of self-discovery, nostalgia, and unfiltered conversations. Discussions moved from fictional characters to personal struggles, memories, and triumphs. And then, one day, a thought emerged-why just read stories when we have so many of our own to tell?

Reclaiming Their Stories

Writing, however, was a different challenge. The women had spent their lives absorbing and critiquing literature, but sharing their own vulnerabilities on paper felt entirely new. Yet, the moment they began, it felt right. Encouragement poured in from friends and family who saw the value in their words. Their motivation grew, transforming what started as a casual idea into something deeply meaningful.

Of course, not everyone was convinced. Some eyebrows raised, amused smiles were exchanged, and the inevitable question arose "A book? Really?" But in the end, conviction triumphed over scepticism. And so, they wrote unapologetically, honestly, and from the heart.

The Essence of This Book

Puchka in the Polders consists of twelve narrations that highlight the power of resilience, the beauty of embracing both tradition and modernity, and the belief that our shared humanity is where true strength lies. These stories reflect the three women's journey of overcoming obstacles, questioning the sometimes-ludicrous societal norms, and finally making a space for themselves. They mock their ignorance of youth and unabashedly celebrate their wins. They share their moments as mothers and wives in a culture greatly distanced from the one at birth. They talk about being the daughter who stays in a foreign land but still upholds the values and expectations of a family back in India.

This book is not about literary excellence or perfect narration; it is instead raw and rustic, with an overdose of emotion. It is an effort to share these women's bittersweet memories with readers who will relate to this effortlessly and with a generation that needs to know these stories to better understand their roots in India.

Beyond Language: A Book for All

This book aims to capture the bittersweet essence of living between cultures.

Each writer expresses herself in the language she feels most comfortable with some narratives are in English, others in Hindi, and some in a blend of both. Instead of translating in any one language, the Hindi narrations are transliterated into Roman script, making them accessible to those who understand the Hindi language but never formally learned the Devanagari script.

This book embraces the humour and beauty of navigating dual cultures, where "What's up?" and *"Kya haal hai?"* coexist effortlessly. It is a celebration of modified authenticity, honouring traditions while evolving with the times. Whether reading in English, Hindi, or Hinglish, this book invites readers to respect cultural nuances, collaborate across linguistic divides, and laugh at the quirks of a world where chai and coffee, Bollywood and Hollywood, Diwali and Christmas exist side by side.

Because in the end, whether you say, "good night" or *"shubh ratri,"* it's all about connection, understanding, and embracing the spaces in between. So, dive in, enjoy the blend, and celebrate a journey that is uniquely yours.

The book is divided into four sections: Time, Age, Food, and Musings, themes that encapsulate their reflections. These broad categories allow the narratives to flow naturally, covering childhood memories, cultural traditions, evolving identities, and deeply personal musings.

A Journey That Continues . . .

Just as the polders symbolize resilience and the ability to shape one's environment, this book is a tribute to those who adapt, redefine, and thrive despite shifting landscapes. And just like puchka, which leaves a lingering taste that makes you crave more, these shared moments will stay with you long after you turn the last page.

In the following pages, each of them will be revealed to you, but before you start, here's a brief sketch of the three writers so that you have some context while going through their life's moments.

This is who they are...

About the Authors

Shayonti Chatterji

The journey of life so far has been exhilarating, challenging, and at times, bewildering - marked by countless highs and lows, moments of darkness and light, splashes of vivid colours mixed with grey. It is this unpredictable rhythm that has kept me moving forward.

At the age of 18, I left the confines of home and family to pursue higher education abroad. After completing my master's in economics and armed with an MBA embarked on a career path that took me to various parts of the world. Over the years I learnt to assimilate with local cultures, adapt to lifestyles, and express myself in foreign languages. Evolving as a global citizen I always remained true to my roots and my philosophy- it gave me strength and conviction to move forward against all odds.

My corporate career spanning over 25 years did reward me with some financial stability but not always the fulfilment I was looking for.

In 2020, I decided to go my way to give fruition to a long-cherished dream- Started my own sustainable lifestyle brand celebrating artisanal craftsmanship from India. My brand is still at its infancy, keeping me up nights but it is mine, a reflection of who I am, what I stand for, and the world I want to create.

My ideal world is where we make a choice simply because it's right, where empathy is always in style, and each of us, despite our differences in race, sex, colour, religion, feel safe and comfortable. As a woman, and a woman of colour there has been many hurdles thrown my way, but I believe in using my voice, my words and carving the space that is denied to me.

Unfolding the chapters of life and looking back I realize today my biggest achievements were to be a mother and a wife. I am the mother of a feisty girl who teaches me every day to sharpen and better my parenting skills.

I am also a wife and my partner, Vikas, has taught me patience, balance, and the importance of seeking the good before the bad. Together, for over three decades we have built a journey of growth and understanding.

❋ ❋ ❋

Reshmi Nashier

If we were to sit down for a conversation, I'd probably begin by sharing where I come from: Pune, where love was unconditional, strength was second nature, and family was everything. My *nani's* warmth, my *maa's* quiet resilience, my dad's unwavering commitment to discipline and the beautiful mess of growing up with four siblings shaped the very core of who I am.

Life wasn't always perfect, but it was in its imperfections that I found grace. That's where I embraced the spirit of *wabi-sabi*, the art of finding beauty in imperfection, and the philosophy of *kaizen*, the quiet, relentless pursuit of growth

My journey took me from the simplicity of village life and the discipline of the army to dual master's degrees in computer science and human resources, followed by over 25 years of experience, including more than four years as a member of a Board of Governor, where I began to see how deeply technology and the human experience are connected.

At my heart, I am an advocate for justice, equity, diversity, inclusion, and belonging (JEDIB), and my purpose is to uplift and empower those around me.

But life isn't just about work, it's also about the adventures that shape us. I find my freedom in running, painting, skydiving, scuba diving, and expressing my thoughts through poetry that speaks to the world's realities.

And through all these adventures, my greatest one is the life I share with my soulmate, Anil Nashier, my *"sabse pyara* punching bag,"* an incredible chief technology officer, and an even better chef. Together, we navigate life's highs and lows, anchored by our two most precious gifts: our daughter, Dr. Chhavi Nashier, my inspiration and favourite person, and our son, Udit Nashier, a pure soul and my favourite cricketer, who fills our days with energy and laughter.

I am also blessed with friendships that span the globe and one four-legged companion, Bruno, whose unconditional love reminds me to stay grounded. Life isn't meant to be perfect, it's meant to be lived, felt, and embraced in all its beautiful chaos. And that's exactly how I choose to live it: with open arms, a full heart, and an unwavering belief in love, growth, and connection.

❋ ❋ ❋

Satya Akhouri

Born into a close-knit family, the eldest of four sisters and a brother, I grew up surrounded by love, laughter, and the gentle weight of responsibility. My childhood was woven across many landscapes of India, as my father's job took us to different places. Each new city was a beautiful, curiosity-filled travel adventure with its own language, customs, and flavours.

I completed my schooling in Delhi and moved to Rajasthan for higher education at a university steeped in Gandhian values. I discovered a life where discipline met adventure, with yoga instilling a sense of mindfulness and strength, and the thrill of horse riding and exhilaration of flying a Cessna telling me that the sky was never the limit. Though I trained as a computer programmer, my heart led me into the world of teaching, where I found joy in shaping young minds, something I continue to enjoy till today.

Marriage took me on a leap of faith across to the Caribbean Island of Curaçao, to a vastly different culture. I never shied away from the excitement life had to offer. I embraced it fully, marvelling at the complete freedom and expression of thoughts of the people there. As I wasn't working, I channelled the creativity inside me and picked up ceramics, where my hands shaped clay into forms that reflected my evolving journey. Painting became my solace, my escape, and my expression. I satiated my adventurous needs through scuba diving. And then came my two greatest creations, my children, who became my pride, my joy, and the most beautiful chapters of my life. Soon after, life carried me once more to a new land, the Netherlands, a land of tulips, polders, canals, it was a place where cultures converged. Here, I met people from all over the world, formed lifelong friendships, and found new ways of creativity to express myself.

No matter how far I travelled, India, with its fragrances of spices, echoes of temple bells, and vibrancy of festivals, always stayed in my heart. Despite my adoption of new foreign cultures, the Indian rhythm remains in my soul and never fades.

Through every chapter of my life, one thing remained constant, my husband, Amod. He is the wind beneath my wings, who always believed in my dreams and encouraged me to move forward, to transform challenges into stepping stones.

I have never been one to dwell on regrets or look back. Instead, I believe in finding solutions, in taking life as it comes, and in moving forward with resilience and grace.

❈ ❈ ❈

Time

समय

Time that is there and the time that has gone by

Time moves on making it almost impossible to keep pace with, and as we grapple to hold on, it rather mischievously slips away. A mother who once held the home together, now waits in quiet longing, her world shrinking to merely a few footsteps, a few fading voices. A daughter races through life, believing there will always be another visit, another moment to talk - until there isn't. A child, once nestled in a grandmother's lap, drifts into adulthood, only to realize too late that home was not just a place, it was an anchor to life, Stories once whispered under starlit skies are now a reflection on a glass screen, choices once made in silence are now debated in voices too loud to hear the past. Nevertheless, love lingers on, through that unexpected hug, in an untouched cup of tea, in a mother's weary eyes that still stays awake waiting for her child to come home. Will we turn back before love becomes only a memory? Will we listen before the silence swallows the words unspoken?

WHEN THERE WAS STILL TIME

A gust of wind pushed the door open as I walked slowly, towards the exit. I couldn't see anything outside, it was difficult to tell whether it was smoke or fog. There was a strange coldness in the air, and at the same time, a faint smell of smoke arose, as if something was smouldering. As I tried to push my way through, a thick white curtain of smoke blinded me, making it impossible to move any farther. I was conscious that I had to go through; there was no way out. I sensed the door was at the end, but I was standing at the edge of an abyss, or what felt like it – a steep fall ahead. What lay at the end of the fall was unknown. I was scared, shaking with fear.

All of a sudden, Ma came from behind. Of late, her walk had become a little unsteady; I could never make out whether it was her knee after the failed operation or her gravely bunioned feet. She walked slowly towards where I was standing. Even though it was physically impossible for her anymore, I felt as if she almost ran forward.

She called out to me in her usual threatening tone, asking me to wait. She darted towards the door with a strength I didn't know she still possessed. With one hand, she pushed me to the ground, and before I could recover from the shock, she had run out through the door, the exit and into the abyss of smoke and fumes. No one really knew what lay at the foot.

I recovered from my panic and suddenly felt a strange calmness around me – a feeling that could almost be mistaken for safety. The worst was over. I was safe and saved.

I arrived in Delhi after almost two long years. The two COVID years had made it impossible to travel – or, now thinking in retrospect, they had given me the perfect alibi for not making my annual trips to meet Ma. I was preoccupied with work and settling my daughter into university. Nici's various career-related issues were high on my priority list. I needed to be there for her. It was a crucial period in her life. She being an only child, I had always been very involved in all her day-to-day matters, and she depended a great deal on us, her parents – to always be there, ever-present.

The day I landed in Delhi after a gap of two years, it was April, and summer in Delhi had already set in. I could feel the heat, humidity, and pollution all rolled into one as we drove from the airport to the house where Ma was now living. For me, home in India had always been synonymous with where my parents resided, not the brick-and-mortar structure that housed them.

Much had happened in the past two years. Ma had suffered a stroke. Though mild, it had taken a heavy toll on her. Ever since the stroke, her once ever-alert nature had changed. She often forgot things, she lost track of time, and sometimes her thoughts were incoherent, her mind wavering. Her recovery was nothing short of a miracle. I had stayed on top of things as much as it was possible from a distance. I was in Amsterdam, and WhatsApp had been our main conduit. She had been confined to the house with her caregiver for two long years, almost never stepping out.

A couple of times, my sister took Ma over to her house to meet the grandchildren and for a change of scenario. But there was never enough time, and it was too much of a hassle given that Ma could barely walk and needed to be carried down the stairs and wheeled around.

It was always a matter of time. Everyone else was busy, while spare time was the one thing she had in abundance at this stage of her life – and the one thing we, her family, were running out of every day.

My trips to India over the last few decades had always been about meeting my parents. Of course, catching up with old friends, endless shopping trips, and aimless walking around the city of my birth were also big parts of the itinerary. Usually, I would go for two and a half to three weeks – the maximum time we could take off in a year. Ma used to wait in anticipation for these trips, and from the day I arrived, she started her countdown. Every few days, she would casually remark how many days were left before my return to Amsterdam. Most times, I would get a little irritated and remind her that all her errands, chores, and household repairs would be taken care of within the remaining days. She would dryly – or perhaps dispassionately – say, 'We hardly get to talk. You are always busy. There is so much I wanted to tell you.'

I always felt that was unfair and somewhat of a selfish remark coming from her, given she had barely ever made a trip to meet her ailing parents. I came to visit them every year without fail and stayed with Ma and Bapi for the entire duration of my stay. I made it a point to be always with them during meals; it was almost like a ritual. I knew family meals were important for them and a means to express their love and care for me. How was it still not enough? Even though Nici would have loved it, I never took time off to tour India. Go to the mountains, the seaside resorts, and all those exotic places the world came to see in India. I stayed in sweltering, polluted Delhi, as I felt that was the only opportunity to spend some time with my parents.

But somehow, it still wasn't enough. Why did they want me to sit at home all day when, after all, I was on a holiday too?

Ma just wanted to sit down and talk. She barely spoke to anyone. Over the years, friends had drifted away, and some had passed on. She was lonely.

It wasn't enough to be cared for and provided with necessities. At this stage of her life, when the horizon was almost at arm's length, her biggest desire was to spend time with her daughters and grandchildren – to be involved in their lives and to feel like an active part of them. But that didn't happen.

We were very different people, and as we grew older, our paths diverged more and more. She was a responsibility and a duty we both siblings took very seriously, especially after Bapi passed away, but she was never truly a friend to me.

My sister and I would often talk about who did exactly what for her, who was quicker at organizing her groceries, taking her for medical check-ups, or refilling her medications. It was as if we were justifying how efficiently we took care of her, scoring brownie points in our minds to compensate for the time we didn't spend with her.

Time. Somehow, it never crossed our minds. We were there for her from a distance, day and night, to ensure all her physical needs were met. Surely that was enough – or was it?

I was tense driving home from the airport. Over the last few months, I had found myself impatient with Ma, sometimes even irritated. I had my own personal matters to take care of, and looking after her from a distance wasn't easy.

I remember her asking me one day, "So, with Corona, will you never come to India again?" Ever since the stroke, her thoughts were sometimes foggy. She didn't fully understand the outside world's situation due to COVID. She knew she couldn't go out and that nobody was coming to visit her as often as before. She was cared for but very alone – a situation she had ungrudgingly accepted.

When I quietly entered the apartment, she was sitting at the dining table, right by the entrance, with her eyes fixed on the door. She was never very expressive, but I felt she was relieved to see me. Relieved might not be the best word, but it was what I read in her eyes when I simply asked, "How are you?" The question felt unnecessary, almost redundant. I had checked on her before boarding the flight. Probably, what I meant to say was, "I'm here now. I'm with you." But neither of us was ever generous in expressing emotions.

No matter how difficult things were for me, no matter how troubled or scared I felt, I always concealed my emotions from her. My vulnerabilities, I thought, would only weaken her. She always looked to me for strength and support.

I stayed for three and a half weeks, the longest I had been in India in decades. There was a lot to be done: repairs, doctor visits, utility arrangements, pest control, settling issues with her caregivers – the list was endless. I tried to at least sit with her during all her meals, even if I wasn't eating with her. Of course, I also spent time with friends, stayed over with them a couple of times, and visited my favourite spots in the city.

No matter how late I returned, she would be awake, waiting for me. I'm not sure if she wanted me to come to her room and sit down to talk, but I would faintly wish her goodnight and head off to bed. It felt as if I was avoiding the unasked questions that had built up over the last two years.

Consciously or not, I avoided acknowledging what I knew she expected of me. It was as if I were trying to distance myself emotionally, hoping she would do the same. Maybe her expectations would lessen, and somehow, she would grow less emotionally dependent on me.

This time, there was no countdown to my departure. She didn't complain about how quickly the days had gone by or how much more she had wanted to do while I was around. In the past, I had often thought that her endless list of chores and errands for me was her way of keeping me entwined in her life – holding on to a bond we both knew had weakened over the years.

This time, as I was about to leave for the airport, she simply seemed scared: scared of the unknown, scared of the inevitable. We both knew it was coming. We just didn't know when.

When I hugged her before leaving, she said quietly, "Don't know when we'll meet again." Little did I know, never again.

It's been two years now since she passed. I'm left with memories – bitter and sweet, and the thought that, if I could do it all over again, I might do things differently.

As a mother myself, I wonder how I missed out on so much that should have been obvious. There were misses at both ends, I know. Until the day I meet her again, I'll always wonder: What if? What if I had done things differently? What if I had just... spent a little more time?

She was there to take the leap into the abyss for me. Will I be able to do the same when my time comes?

*S*leep
       Would not come while she sat nursing the infant me

Sleep stayed away as she lay awake nights nursing the sick child.

She was sleepless as she helped her infant flourish to childhood

Anxiously she stayed awake while I was out having just a good time.

Sleep wouldn't come as she lay awake helpless while I struggled in my adult world.

Sleep

At last she is fast asleep

Nothing will wake her anymore

Sleep now rests heavily on her tired eyes

Sleep, sweet sleep she has been awake too long.

Shayonti Chatterji

WAT KOMT, VERDWIJNT MET DE HORIZON

WHAT COMES DISAPPEARS WITH THE HORIZON

Do the ends of a river ever truly meet? Water transforms as it journeys, changing in shape and taste, mingling with whatever it encounters, at times the purest, at times tainted, only to find its way back to purity. The river flows forward, unbothered by time, embracing Evolution. Stories, too, are written in one moment and woven in another. My journey began on July 12, 1975, in Pune Cantt, and now, fifty years later, I find myself writing it in the Netherlands. It feels as if I am sitting at the river's midpoint, flowing through all its experiences while looking back at where it all began. But do the ends of a river ever truly meet?

Vivid memories blur the lines between dream and reality. My earliest years were spent in my *pyaari Nani's* home, my beloved grandmother, where I was showered with love. Being an overweight newborn, my mother was advised not to carry me, as the family still hoped for a male child. Not out of disregard, but simply because, in those days, that was the way society was shaped. Sons carried the family name forward, while daughters, after marriage, often took on a new surname and joined another household. It was seen as tradition, and I must admit, there was a certain grace to it when not distorted into a measure of worth or power. I still cherish the sentiment of that tradition when it was held with love, and not as a hierarchy of gender.

But as the river flowed, somewhere along the way, it started to be seen differently, less as a societal rhythm and more as a system of imbalance, giving weight to one and invisibility to the other.

Those first four years were filled with endless stories from my Nana, playful days in the fields with cousins, and the warmth of my three aunts, and cattle. The innocence of childhood made me believe that this was the world, complete, whole, and unchanging despite the perceived hardships of village life.

It was not that everything was perfect. There were things I didn't enjoy or connect with. I somehow had the faith that when things would be in my control, I would at least try to work on them, or make sure I don't pass them on to the next generation. And if there's one thing I know for sure, it's that I learned how to make choices, like the river, brushing past the edges before moving on and disappearing with time.

But by the time I learned to speak, the place I had called home, where I felt I belonged, became nothing more than a summer retreat. The permanence I once believed in was suddenly fleeting And still, somehow, I was fine, drifting through it all like a river that knows its way. Maybe it was love. Not just the love that found me, but the love I quietly held for myself, the kind that comes from simply being alive, from noticing the warmth in a passing touch, the silent support in a glance, the unspoken gestures that wrapped around me like soft threads of belonging. I chose to anchor myself in those moments, not in the absences, the unanswered questions, or the need for acknowledgment. Life shifted, reshaped itself without warning, but I moved with it. There were struggles, yes, layers of emotion, the ache of delayed choices, but something deeper kept whispering, you'll be fine... your time will come. So I learned to meet joy with open arms, and greet sorrow by going inward, imprinting those unclaimed dreams into my blood, my breath, my being, so that when the time arrives, they will rise not as wishes, but as a life fully lived, in my own voice, on my own terms..

Now, I was considered lucky instead of unlucky, just because my brother was born after me. I am still unsure if I truly felt that way, or if it was really true. Even now, I keep asking myself, was it real, or just something I convinced myself of?

I think when I was four, I permanently moved from the village to my Maa's home in the city, accompanied by my nani. I entered the house, confused and bewildered, not knowing exactly what this new world was. I quietly took refuge behind the curtains. Suddenly, a hand tapped me from the back as if to say, You are safe. You are home too.

That simple touch made me realize I was among loved ones, even in this unfamiliar place. This was a house filled with my mother, three sisters, a brother, and my army-wale papa. I was a girl from a village, now living in a home with a sister in a convent school, two other academically brilliant sisters, and a brother who was adored by all. It felt like a world so different from what I had known.

The simplicity of my village life seemed so far away in this new world. Nicknamed Hardy, my father was the epitome of style and elegance, his boots polished to a gleam, his uniform crisp and sharp, his presence commanding in olive green. And my Maa, draped in her saree with a bindi, was adored by all. That bindi, my dad's favourite, has been missing since 2006. And then there was me, just a little girl, trying to make sense of it all, still peeking from behind the curtains.

Slightly scary, slightly anxious, slight fear of acceptability, and a spice of strange confidence, I learned the ways of a new life, a bumpy ride. Dining table took the place of my Nani's lap; bohiya (casserole) and kadai changed to plates and cutlery. Ram ram turned into good morning, good night. Slightly scary, slightly anxious, slight fear of acceptability and a spice of strange confidence, I learned all the manners, yet a bumpy ride. It wasn't about finding a place to sit on the floor; it was more about finding the space I was in and the manners that came with it.

It would be wrong to say that I felt the same belonging, which was there in the aangan of Ranila village, saal(living room) of Shri Girdhari lal's Ghar, though sometimes lost in trying to understand them, sometimes blended effortlessly. Despite very much feeling the living ghosts in the Oobra(Storage room) even today....

As years rolled by, I settled in my new home, and I began enjoying the moments with my siblings. We had our fun ways of making the most of the time.

But was this permanent? Strangely enough, no. My elder sisters got married and left home; so did I. Moving to a new home, taking a new surname, stepping into a completely different environment with a new maa and new paa, my in-laws' family. Back to eating from one plate, sitting on the floor. Here, everyone enjoyed food with their hands. From enjoying rich, indulgent dishes, I returned to the simplicity of satvik food.

I was in my new room, and a kiss on my forehead revived the same feeling that the girl behind the curtains felt: cared for and loved. Slightly scary, slightly anxious, slight fear of acceptability, and a spice of strange confidence, I learned all the ways of a married life, a beautiful roller coaster

Then, as life unfolded, during my first pregnancy, a few days before my due date, my water bag burst, and I was advised to wait till my labour pains set in. Two days later, the labour pains started, and my daughter had to be brought out into the world through forceps delivery. When I anxiously held my newborn, the reassuring touch on my head by the gynaecologist brought back the same feeling as the kiss on my forehead and the tap on my shoulder; it was the feeling of warmth and confirmation that everything is fine. I was glad that I was advised to wait, because had I not, I would have missed that touch on my forehead. Sometimes, the beauty of what lies ahead depends entirely on what unfolds in the present moment.

Slightly scary, slightly anxious, slight fear of responsibility, and a spice of strange confidence,

I learned the ways of a new life, being a maa myself.

When I became a maa, I found myself doing all the things my Nani and Maa did, waking up in the middle of the night, worrying over a simple sneeze of Chhavi, using all the desi Nuskah (remedies) for any illness, with a shift of cherishing all her firsts: first tooth, first word, first roll, first steps, first visit to the park, first vaccination, early childhood school, and first cycle lessons. And before I knew it, my second-born arrived, and my mother, sitting in her chair, was once again knitting little socks, just like my Nani. I witnessed the ends of the river meeting.

I began to realize that what comes does not disappear with the horizon; it changes form but is seen in different ways, in actions, in learning, in decisions. It is not consciously that we learn; it is the time that teaches us. The power of the unconscious mind and heart. I found my way through the quiet yet powerful gestures of love, the tap on my shoulder, the kiss on my forehead, the gentle caress on my head. As humans, in our most challenging moments, all we truly seek is a sense of belonging. The realization, or rather, the art of being present, becomes paramount in overcoming the trials life places before us. The essence of existence lies in the choices we make, choices like the one my maa made when she entrusted her own mother to provide me with a safe and loving home, even in her absence.

Today, I understand the weight of that decision, the strength it must have taken for her to let her daughter be raised far away. In my own journey, I, too, made choices - to adapt, to navigate between modernity and tradition, to embrace the ebb and flow of change. And Then came the choice to become a maa myself, surrendering my peace to the tiny yet profound moments, like anxiously awaiting my child's timely poop.

Like a river flowing through forests and cities, my life has moved through stillness and storm, village roots, urban rhythms, and all in between. Each bend left its mark, but a quiet thread of care always held. It taught me to sift the pain, hold the grace, and move forward with what keeps my spirit light and my conscience joyful.

Sometimes, it is the seemingly insignificant decisions that carve the path of our lives, shaping not only our personal stories but also the world we inhabit. Life moves forward, and we, too, must move with it. We cannot hold on to the past, nor can we slow down time. But perhaps, in recognizing its rhythms, in listening closely to the whispers of existence, we find the clarity to make choices that extend beyond ourselves, shaping the world around us. I wonder if we truly realize the shifts we create, consciously or unconsciously, in the world we live in. Should we simply focus on our own lives, or should we prepare for the transformations the future will bring. From large joint families to smaller nuclear units, from raising many children to raising one or two, perhaps even choosing adoption exclusively.

Our choices define the generations that follow. When I look at the world today, at the balance between population and resources, the growing urgency of sustainability, and the struggles of children in third-world countries, I can't help but ask: Are we moving towards something greater? In a time where we label generations as Gen X, Gen Y, and Gen Z, reducing our identities to mere alphabets, could it be that Mother Earth, in her wisdom, or some divine presence, is guiding us towards a necessary shift?

We have choices. And the choices we make today will shape the world of tomorrow.

We live, we love, we choose, hoping that something good outlasts us. Not everything needs to be seen to be felt, or finished to be complete. For what comes, disappears with the horizon and sometimes, that is enough. And sometimes, it stays in a word remembered, a value lived, a kindness passed on quietly anchoring the lives that follow.

Shaant Nadi Kehti Hai | Zindagi Bahti Hai ||
Milna Hai Samundar Se, Kab Kaha Maine?

Mitaana Hai Astitv Ko, Kab Chaha Maine?

Behana Niyam Hai Prakriti Ka | Niyam Hi Rehne Do ||

Shaant Nadi Kehti Hai | Zindagi Bahti Hai ||

Cheerna Hai Chataano Ko, Kab Chaha Maine?

Aana Hai Toofan Ko, Kab Chaha Maine?

Sangharsh Niyam Hai Prakriti Ka | Niyam Hi Rehne Do ||

Simatata Hai Sabhi Kuch Mujh Mein, Kiya Kya Maine?

Har Rang Mein Dhali Main, Paya Kya Maine?

Aalingan Niyam Hai Prakriti Ka | Niyam Hi Rehne Do ||

Shaant Nadi Kehti Hai | Zindagi Bahti Hai ||

Baadal Ki Boond Parvat Par, Kab Buni Maine?

Jagah Vasundhara Par Apni, Kahan Buni Maine?

Jeevan Niyam Hai Prakriti Ka | Niyam Hi Rehne Do ||

Kahan Saagar Mein Mili, Kab Chuna Maine?

Naam Kab Kho Gaya, Kab Jaana Maine?

Mrityu Niyam Hai Prakriti Ka | Niyam Hi Rehne Do ||

Shaant Nadi Kehti Hai | Zindagi Bahti Hai ||

Shaant Nadi Bahti Hai | Zindagi Kehti Hai ||

Reshmi Nashier

✹ ✹ ✹

***

Virasat ka Safar, is the next narration about the passage of Time. Time that refuses to slow down and take a break while we play catch up. It has been transliterated from its original Hindi version because a translation can never do justice to the tug-of-heart between a mother and daughter. 'Mamma, kahan kho gayi aap?'

Aage aap khud hi padh le............

***

Virasat ka Safar

Apni maa ke saath unke ghar ke dining table par baith garam "masala chai" ki chuskiyon ke beech unki bachpan ki kahaniyan sun rahi thi. Bahar halki thand thi par chai me pade adrak aur ilaichi se sharir me ek garmahat thi. Ya shayad ye garmahat maa ke ghar me hone matr se hi thi? Purani yadon ki khushboo hawa mein ghuli hui thi. Us samay ki jab jeevan ek alag gati se aage chalti thi aur paramparayein gehri jaden jamaye hui thi.

"Humare dino mein..." maa ki aawaz yadon mein kho gayi, "humare paas toh ye sabhi gadgets nahi the, hum sab bhai behan chhat par taaron ke neeche baith laalten ki roshni me pushton se chali aa rahi kahaniyan suna karte the. Waise bhi jis parivaar mein nau bhai-behan hon, wahan kahaniyon aur kisse ki koi kami nahi thi, ya to bade kuch kehte, ya chhote kuch sunate"

Main kai baar doharai hui is kahani ko bade dhyan se sun rahi thi par mera dimag paas ke pade hue smartphone ki chamakti screen ki aur kheench gaya jis par meri beti se notifications aa rahe the.

Apni maa ki peedhi aur apni beti ke peedhi ke beech ke antar ko mehsoos karte hue ek halki si muskurahat chehre par bikhar gayi.

Itne mein meri beti bhagti hui kamre mein aayi. Uski ankhen utsah aur khushi se paripurn thi. Usne mujhe gale lagate hue kaha, "Mumma mujhe apni pasandida college mein admission mil gaya hai, ab main wahan ja kar journalism padhhungi."

Meri maa garv se muskurayi lekin unki aawaz mein avishwas ka sanket tha. "Journalism? Jahan kahaniyan likhna sikhate hain? Agar wo padhne me acchi hai to phir medicine aur engineering kyon nahi?" Unke liye ye sapna kuch ajnabi tha. Apni duniya se bilkul alag duniya mein apni nati ke uplabdhi ka mahatva samajhne ke liye bada sangharsh karte hue unhone poocha.

"Haan maa," main doh peedhiyon ki doori ko kam karne ke liye dakhal dete hue boli. "Woh lekhan ke madhyam se khud ko abhivyakt karna chahti hai. Uska rasta alag hai par utna hi vaidhya aur santosh janak hai."

Apni maa ki paaramparik parvarish aur apni beti ki adhunik akankshao ke beech ke antar ko dekh bada ashcharya hua.

Ek madhya vargiya parivar mein paanch bhai behanon mein sabse badi thi main. Jaisa ki 70 ke dashak mein hota tha, zyadatar madhyavargiya parivar mein padhai ko sabse zyada ahmiyat di jaati thi. Papa ki kamai ka shayad sabse bada hissa humare school fees mein hi jata tha. Paanch bachhon ki akele kamai par parvarish karna aasan toh nahi raha hoga. Dilli mein rehne ke kaaran aksar rishtedaron ka aana jaana laga rehta tha. Aisa koi din mujhe yaad nahi, jis din sirf hum bhai behan aur mummy papa ghar par akele baith kar khana khate the. Koi na koi ghar par jaroor aaya hua hota. Ya toh koi padhai ke liye aaya hota, toh koi naye college me admission lene ke liye, koi apne acche doctor se ilaj karwane ke liye ya toh koi apni hawa pani badalne ke liye. Kai baar toh humari garmi chhuttiyon ka plan bhi is kaaran nahi ban paya. Bachpan se hi aisa dekha tha toh ye samanya lagta tha. Sab kuch sabka hota tha chahe wo kapde hon ya kamra. Privacy ka toh humne kabhi naam hi nahi suna tha. Sara kaam ka bhaar maa par aata aur woh aksar is baat se khush nahi hoti, par unki khushi ko nazarandaz kar diya jata.

Aise hi maa bachhon ki parvarish aur ghar sambhalne mein aur papa apne kaam mein vyast rehte. Kaam ke silsile mein papa aksar desh videsh jaate. Maine kabhi maa ko papa ke saath kahin jaate hue nahi dekha. Maa ka mann to karta hi hoga par parivarik aur aarthik zimmedariyon ne kabhi yeh vichar unke mann se bahar aane hi nahi diya.

Mujhe ek kissa bahut hi saaf yaad hai, main kareeb solah saal ki rahi hongi aur dashvi kaksha me padhti thi. Papa ko ek baar apne kaam ke silsile se ek saal se zyada videsh mein rehne ke liye jaana tha. Hum sab bhai behan bade khush the ki hum sab hawai jahaz mein baithkar videsh jayenge, par nishchay yeh hua ki hum sab mummy ke saath yahin rahenge aur papa akele hi jayenge. Bhala tenth ke board ke samay koi doosre school jaata hai? Na toh humse puchha gaya aur na hi humari rai li gayi. Maa baap ne apna faisla sunaya aur humne usey sweekar kar liya. Udaas to hum sab hue par humne apne maa papa ke faisle ko sahi maana.

Waqt kitna badal gaya hai! Aaj jab apne bachhon se baat karti hoon to har faisle mein unka drishti kon hota hai, phir chaahe wo khane mein kaun si sabzi khani hai ya college mein kaun se subjects padhne hai. Apne vicharo ko vyakt karne ki swatantrata ko kitna mahatva dete hai aur avashyak maante hain!

Aksar yeh sochti hoon ki kya hum mein sochne samajhne ki shakti nahi thi? Kyun hum har decision ko bina tark ke maan lete the? Humara samajik vatavaran aur paramparik parvarish aisi thi ki agar koi bada, chahe woh mata pita ho ya koi rishtedar ya phir humare shikshak, kuch kahe toh hum usey bina discussion ke sweekar kar lete the. Umar mein bada hone se hi toh koi hamesha sahi nahi hota?

Humari udaasi toh kuch dinon ki hi thi jo ki papa ke jaane ke baad wapas dincharya mein aate hi kho gayi. Humein bas ab intezar rehta tha tarah-tarah ke naye kapde aur tohfe jo papa foreign se laate. Ek saal poora kar papa wapas aaye. Ghar mein khushi ka thikana nahi tha, ek toh papa wapas aa gaye aur doosra Dussehra ka tyohar jo aaya tha.

Tyoharon ka intezar poore ghar parivar ko rehta tha. Hum sab bhai behan kuch na kuch karne mein vyast rehte. Kahin koi rangoli bana raha hota to koi aam ke patte darwaze par laga raha hota. Maa ka toh ek hi kaam tha, woh tarah-tarah ke pakwan banati. Har tyohar ke saath alag-alag tarah ke pakwan aur mithaiyan thi jo banaye jaate. Do teen din pehle se hi saari tayariyan shuru ho jaati. Rishtedaron ka aana jaana laga rehta aur school college mein chutti hone ke kaaran bachhon per padhai ka bojh bhi nahi hota. Humare ghar naye kapde sirf do hi tyohar par kharide jate, Dussehra aur Holi. Hum khushi se phoolen nahi samate the.

Dukan jaakar naye kapde kharidna aur tyohar ke din woh kapde pehan kar ithlana. Tyohar ke din aksar rishtedar aur paas-padosi humare ghar aate, aur apne ghar banayi hui mithai aur namkeen ek doosre ko dete. Paanch bhai-behan ka ghar hone ke kaaran koi bhi mithai ya pakwan humare ghar mein jyada der tak tikti nahi thi, jo bhi cheez aati jald hi khatam ho jaati.

Aaj jab videsh mein reh kar koi tyohar manati hoon toh na toh saara desh woh tyohar mana raha hota hai aur na hi school office mein chutti hoti hai. Jo bachhe jab marzi naye kapde kharidte hai, unhe tyohar par naye kapdo ka mahatva kya pata? Kai baar toh mausam bhi saath nahi deta. Jaise bhala zero degree tapman mein holi ka kya mazaa? Aise mein tyohar manana bada hi atpata sa lagta hai. Tyohar manane ka mahol hi nahi hota. In sab halaat ke bawajood maine tyoharon ko hamesha utne hi utsah aur khushi ke saath apne parivar aur doston ke saath manaya. Is aasha aur vishwas ke saath ki kal jab mere bachhe apne bachpan mein jhake toh unhe bhi in tyohar mein bitaye hue ye khushi ke pal phir se in tyoharon ko manane ki prerna de.

Kaafi barson ke baad mujhe yeh ehsaas hua ki humare mata-pita ne kitna bada balidan diya tha. Dono ne akele rehne ka nirnay kiya taki bachhon ki padhai mein kuch adchanein na aayein aur kuch paise bach payein jisse unka bhavishya ujjwal ho sake. Unke is balidaan ne hum sab par kahin na kahin apni chhap chhodi hai. Jo kuch seekha apne maa-baap se seekha chahein woh balidan ki bhavna ho ya apne paraye ki madad ya seva karna ki.

Isliye aksar apne apko buzurg mata-pita ki zimmedari aur apne bachhon ki parwarish ke beech mein phasa hua paati hoon. Apne dayitvon ke beech santulan banane mein badi dikkaton ka samna karti hoon. Na to mata-pita ko bharpoor samay de pati hoon aur na hi bachhon ko. Kya pata ki iska asar mata-pita ke sehat par bhi pad raha ho?

Mata-pita ki bhautik zarooraton ko bhale hi poora karne mein saksham rahoon magar unke bhavnatmak zarooraton ko poora karne mein apne aap ko asamarth paati hoon. Us parinde ko unmukt aasman mein udta hua dekh mann mein aksar ye khayal aata hai ki kaash mere paas bhi ek hasin pankh ka joda hota to jab mera mann karta main bhi ek daal se dusre daal par pal mein uud paati, kabhi apne maa-baap ke paas apne bachpan ke ghar toh kabhi apni shaadi ke baad basaya hua ghar parivar.

Jahan meri maa ki duniya parivarik moolyon aur paramparik bhoomikaon ke ird-gird ghoomti hai, wahi meri beti ke sapne samajik apekshaon se pare apne vyaktigat vikas aur aatmabhivyakti ki ichha se prerit hain.

"Mumma, kahan kho gayi aap? Aap ki chai toh bilkul thandi ho gayi. Main aapke aur nani-ma ke liye phir se chai bana kar laati hoon". Meri beti ne mujhe halke se hilate hue muskurakar kaha.

Ek ne mujhe janam diya aur ek ko maine janam diya. Apni maa aur beti ko saath dekh kar main abhari hoon un yadon ke liye jo humein sadiyon se jodti hain. Unki jeevan shaili aur vichardharon mein asamanataon ke bawajood ek atoot bandhan hai jo samay se pare hai. Pyaar, samman aur saanjha anubhavon se judha ek bandhan jo parivar ki virasat ko aakar deta hai.

Waqt ki chhaon mein

Maa ki rasoi mein ubalti chaay,
Beete waqt ki sunehri parchhaay.

"Hamaare zamaane mein ...." kehte kehte,

Wo laut jaati hai taaron bhari chhat ke neeche.

Main,

Wo madhya ki kadi,

Maa ki mamta aur

Beti ke sapno ke beech khadi.

Ab sochti hoon,

Kab beet gaya wo waqt,

Jab maa ne apni baahon mein thaam rakha tha,

Ab udti hai wo nanhi si chidiya,

Jise kal tak maine sambhaal rakha tha.

Beti daudti hai apni raah par,

Lekar samay ki tez udaan,

Aankhon mein apne khwabon ki pehchan.

Main muskurati hoon,

Par aankhen bhar aati hain,

Kyonki jaanti hoon,

Ki maa ne jo waqt diya,

Wohi meri beti ke aaj ka aadhaar bana.

Waqt ki ret mutthi se fisalti rahi,

Par maa ki baatein man mein jamti rahi.

Waqt ....

Jo maa ki mamta mein dhalta gaya,

Meri samajh mein palta gaya,

Aur beti ki udaan mein udta gaya.

Na koi shikayat,

Na koi gila,

Bas ek sukoon mila,

Waqt ki chhaon mein.

Satya Akhouri

❋ ❋ ❋

Aging

जीवन संध्या

THE REFLECTIONS IN THE MIRROR

Aging flows like a silent river, unnoticed, until the mirror begins to whisper its truth. Shadows of laughter and sorrow weave themselves into delicate lines, silver strands shimmer like moonlight upon restless waves, and the face staring back carries echoes of yesterday. When the number no longer matches the energy within, the desires, the longings, aging becomes unsettling. And then, one day, the lines on the hands seem to trace their way from the hands of our elders, carrying not just age, but memories, lessons, and quiet realizations.

Beyond the mirror's quiet revelation, aging casts its deeper spells. Parents grow frail, their voices softer, their presence more precious. Friendships, once unbreakable, thin like autumn mist, and silence settles where laughter once danced. The past breathes in quiet spaces, and absence carves its mark on the soul. Then comes a moment when the calls from home bring a fleeting hesitation, an unspoken fear of the news they may carry.

Yet, aging is not a loss but a privilege, a gift denied to many far too soon. Every wrinkle is a testament to a life lived, every grey streak a lesson learned. A journey beyond mere years, an unfolding of wisdom wrapped in time's embrace.

It is not about fading but about becoming, not an end but an evolution. The body may slow, but the spirit remains untamed, burning with desires and dreams, some fulfilled, others still waiting in the wings.

So let the mirror whisper, let the years weave their magic, and let the spirit rise, untethered and eternal, burning with the light of all that has been and all that is yet to come. Mere time cannot stop the rising spirit which will wring out much more than what time ever wanted to give.

That Face in the Mirror

It all seems so far away now and, in some ways, even a little odd and strange, as if that me has changed with time. Years back, right after school, a student at the university – I was always in a rush to grow up. On my eighteenth birthday, I recall saying, 'Well, I have completed the eighteenth, so technically, it's the nineteenth year.' I distinctly remember Liza, my roommate, a few years senior to me, jokingly commenting, 'Where are you hurrying to?' She probably had more sense not to rush towards the years to come.

Aging or age was never a concern. If anything, I was indeed rushing, in a hurry to grow up – probably because I had, very early in life, taken up responsibilities beyond my age. Even though I had not reached the number in years, I felt the need to be there to justify what life threw at me. There was a lot to be done and, in those days, the late eighties, life's milestones were somewhat linked to age.

We have all heard the cliché: age is just a number. Hell, NO! It's more than a number. It's an experience, it's a journey, it's a feeling, and it's what, in some ways, defines us as individuals. Maybe a little more so for women than men. I have always wondered why men seem to be invincible in the battle with age. Or is it just a figment of my mind that they are too proud to accept it?

A sultry Moscow summer day I was in a bus; they were never the most comfortable means of travel in those days. The crowd, the lack of any air conditioning, just a few half-open windows for respite, and the Russians incessantly complaining about the heat. One would expect that, after seven months of severe winter, they would welcome the two or three months of summer. But we humans are always myopic, never seeing the bigger picture – instead, reacting to the minor discomforts of the moment at hand.

I was sitting next to an elderly Russian lady, oversized, sweaty,and almost squashing me against the window, as she had even taken up half of my seat. She looked like a friendly soul and tolerable, in spite of her size and profuse sweating. She engaged with me, a small, inconspicuous brown girl from India, in casual conversation, which became an endless chatter. The journey was long, and I continued to indulge her to break the monotony of the arduous ride. The bus jolted to a halt at a stop and a lady stepped in, middle-aged, maybe in her fifties, dressed ever so brightly that almost all heads turned as she pushed her way towards our seat and stood right next to my companion in travel. I don't exactly remember her attire, it was decades ago, but I distinctly recall that everything about her was way too garish and cheap. The clothes were awfully bright, tearing at the seams, a plunging blouse trying to show the cleavage of a pair of sagging breasts. Bleached hair with the grey roots exposed, green eye shadow and a bright red lipstick – everything about her was kind of mismatched, forced upon. Even the cheap perfume she had obviously splashed generously was more of a disturbing stink than a smell. As she stood there glaring at passengers, who glared back, my co-traveller, the elderly lady, turned to me and, without even an effort to lower her voice, said, *'Zensheni umeraet dvazde- pervaya eta biologicheski smert, btoraya korgda ana panimaet shto ni komy ne nuzen.'* 'A woman dies twice – once is the biological death, and the other is when she realises she is not desired as a woman anymore.'

It is over two decades and a little more since this incident, but what the elderly woman said that day remained engraved in my mind unconsciously, though at that moment, in the prime of my youth, in my twenties, I had laughed it off. To me, the brightly dressed lady was no more than someone overdressed in bad taste. As if everything on her was a mismatch.

Mismatch – that's the key word I overlooked when talking about aging. Age is surely a number, but it needs to match with the very being of the individual. When this number fails to match her mood, her energy levels, her desires, and her sensuality, she feels the pangs of age. Aging then becomes a version of herself she feels unsettled about.

In my twenties, when I was rushing to grow up, I was completely indifferent towards aging. It was a distant concept which seemed so, so far away. I was this fearless, confident, too-full-of-myself individual who believed in living on her terms and expected the world to follow. I was always sympathetic towards the elderly and infirm, though inwardly, I felt it wouldn't touch me, and I was somewhat sure that when it did, I could give it the slip.

I slowly entered my thirties and forties. I became a wife and a mother. I grew even older, but somehow the burden of age never dawned upon me – or maybe I never felt it on the supple mass of bones and flesh which was my sinew and one that I was very proud of. Though my roles changed in life, inwardly, I remained the very same, that carefree girl in a smelly Moscow bus.

Growing up, clothes, attire, and accessories to complement the outward appearance were honestly very minor or even non-existent components of my daily life. I even felt awkward and out of place when girlfriends would be discussing clothes, make-up, and hairstyles. To me, it was all just banter which I didn't want to be part of, as I felt it questioned my cerebral component. Why it was the case, I have no idea, but if I try to delve further within, I think it was partly because I comfortably accepted my physical (shortcomings) attributes: short, plump, bespectacled. There was not much I could do about these characteristics except blame my genetic inheritance, so I embraced them and felt pretty content. From a very young age and into my late adulthood, I chose a style simple, comfortable, somewhat classical, and subdued. I felt it helped me blend in amongst the superlatives in a room. Looks and appearance were never my strong point; it was always my highly opinionated mind and my immense confidence to walk in and stand apart in a room full of people. It was always cerebral. The rest seemed frivolous.

But somehow, one day, all that changed...........

Peering into the mirror and looking at myself was not something I was very fond of. I either became too critical of myself, and that somewhat disturbed me, or I would be too smug with the reflection in the mirror, and that didn't seem right.

One fine day (just like the opening of a fairy tale, 'Once upon a time', only this was not to be a fairy tale), I looked into the mirror while applying make-up and noticed a strange fold on the skin in the area between my nose and upper lip, or maybe it was around the mouth. This new feature on my facial geography was unsettling. First, I thought it was a pillow wrinkle or some smudged foundation, but it didn't take me long to realize it was the first wrinkle (or the first I noticed) on flawless skin which had never seen so much as a pimple or a blemish. Things changed a little from that day on. I started noticing things I had never seen before: the crow's feet between my brows, the not-so-even forehead, the unwanted ridges around my mouth. I was visibly aging.

My body was playing tricks, as if it had a mind of its own and I had no control over it. It was reshaping the contours of this structure, my body, which for so long had been mine. Age was now hell-bent on imprinting its presence, irrespective of my consent.

The days, months, and years rolled on, and I saw myself change a little every day. As more and more signs of aging appeared on my physical self, I found myself behaving in a way almost unknown to me. Skincare, makeup, hairstyling, and many acts once considered frivolous all of a sudden became prominent parts of my daily routine. Each time I would look into a mirror, I felt something amiss, and I wanted to improve on my physical attributes. Sagging skin, strands of grey, unwanted creases and folds, furrows and fine lines were constant reminders of years gone by.

Instead of me racing towards the years, I found myself counting the many lived already.

Mismatch was the main culprit. My inner self had not changed much from the girl in her twenties travelling in that smelly Moscow bus. The longings, the desires, the aspirations, and the wants were just as demanding, vibrant, and alive as they were then. I still admired the opposite sex, and I hoped I could turn a few eyeballs towards me when I walked into a room, but each time I looked into the mirror, I felt there was something not really matching up.

I was at a juncture in my journey when probably I needed to act differently, leave the frolics behind, and adorn a different mask upon the aging face.

Each time I try to comprehend this duality, a voice from within whispers to remind me what all remains to be done, and that time is running out.

But then, whenever did time alert us it was coming to an end? Wasn't it always that it would stop suddenly? And if that's the case, should I be even bothered? Should I slow down living life? Or is it that there is still so much more to do, so many more dreams to fulfil, so many battles to fight, and so much more to see that it scares me to see my face, which shows signs of a fading youth and shamelessly heralds age, as if to mock me, daring me to take age head-on before it all comes to a halt?

I do not want to walk. I want to run; I want to be heard; I want to be loud; I want to be bright; I want to matter; I want so much more. Mere time will not stop me, as I shall wring out much more than what time ever wanted to give.

With every passing day, as I stand in front of the mirror, the face that looks back is changing – a change that does not appeal to me; a change that is beyond my control. I struggle to comprehend and accept the inevitable that is age and embrace it with all my heart. Each line, each fold is a testament to my unique journey – an embellishment which none other can have.

My co-traveller in the bus that day was wrong, for I shall die only once – the day breath is robbed of me!

Hop skip jump
        Jump skip hop

Hairs flying, skirts flying

I fly oh so high

I fall with a thud on the ground so hard

I cry so loud in a safe embrace

Spin twirl leap

Leap twirl spin

Hairs flying skirts flying

Eyes peeping, fingers pointing

I fall with a thud on the ground so hard

I cry so loud in a world so cold

I fear so much, I look all around

Think drift sink

Sink drift think

The mind flies high, the mind goes back

I fall with a thud on the ground so hard

I cry so loud I feel so alone

I see no one, I look all around

Shayonti Chatterji

❋ ❋ ❋

***

The last piece on aging was in English. This one? Same soul, new language, Hindi, written just the way we speak it every day, in Roman script. Seedha dil se, no frills, no filters. Just glimpses of aging, the kind that slips in between laughter, a missed thought, or that familiar "kya bolne aayi thi main?"

Toh aaram se padho, mehsoos karo... Aur jahan dil ko halka sa chhoo jaaye, wahan ek muskaan de dena, ya apni koi purani yaad ya kisaa dohra lena.

***

SIMATTHEE JHURIYAAN

Nana-Nani, Dada-Dadi aur unke haathon ki jhurhiyaan. Kaash! Yahin tak seemit hota budhaapa. Samajh nahin paa rahi hoon, Nani ke haath ki jhuriyaan mere haathon par kaise? Kahaan wo din the, jab ghanton jhuriyon ko sahlate hue, Nani ki kahaniyaan sunte the, aur ab aalam yeh hai ki apne haath mein jhurhiyon ki halki si jhalak bhi dikh jaaye, to kahani badal jati hai nuskhon mein, aur khushi kho jaati hai chinta mein. Meree Jhuriyaan Nana Nani kii kahaniyaan dhakne lagi hain.

Woh kahaniyaan, jo kabhi neend ki chadar oḍha deti thin, Ab khud yaadon ki silwaṭon mein simaṭne lagi hain. Aaine mein ubharti lakiroṅ mein main aksar bachpan ḍhūnḍhtī hoon. Woh tulsi ke niche baiṭhkar, Nana ke kandhon par baithe, yahaan wahan ghoomte phirte, sunee hazaaron seekh, Jise woh har baar dheere se kisi kisse mein lapet dete the. Ab jab baalon mein safedi har subah thodi aur pakki ho jaati hai, to lagta hai waqt ka chakr wapas wahin le ja raha hai jahan se sab shuru hua tha. Jhuriyon sai ḍhaktī yaadein aur rishte aur bhi zyada anmol lagte hain. Dhalti umr ki taraf, main har din thoda aur jhukti hoon - na kamzori se, balki un yaadon ka-Pyaar lekar jo kabhi mere jeevan ka aadhar thin.

2021 mein maa joh ussamay 65 sai upper thee, Shayad, unsai hui baatcheet mein ageing ka nichod tha. Us din, maa ke sath dopahar ke samay, ek saath naashta karne ke baad, main aur maa yun hi puraani yaadein taaza kar rahe the, tabhi maa ne kaha, "Jab main kahin baahar jaati hoon aur family group mein apni photo share karti hoon, to tum sab kehte ho, 'bahut sundar lag rahi ho!', par mujhe aisa nahin lagta. Mujhe apni skin, apna rang, apna sa nahin lagta. Kabhi-kabhi sochti hoon, bacche yun hi khush karne ke liye keh rahe hain." Aaj 2025 mein sheeshe ke ek taraf baithi thi main, aur doosri taraf dikh rahi thi meri maa. Jhurrhiyaan kuch kehti, makeup ke baad aaina kuch aur kehta. Sach hai, ageing ke saath halka sa seham jaati hoon.

Kabhi-kabhi hum khud ageing ka anubhav karte hain, aur kabhi-kabhi doosron ki anjaane mein kahi baat iska ehsaas karaati hai. Aisa hi ek kissa meri didi ke ghar mein hua. Kuch saal pehle, meri didi ke ghar Holi ki hudang, har koi safed, peele rangon mein sarābor. Kahin dhol, kahin DJ, kahin uchhalte rang. Khane ki to baat hi mat karo, muh mein paani aa jaata hai. Wahin ek kone mein didi ki ek saheli ko maine namaste kiya, aur wo muskura kar boli, "Bahut sundar lag rahi ho, safed suit, seedhe baal kaafi acche lag rahe hain, bilkul Sumita lag rahi ho. " Sochti hoon, kya wo sach mein taarif thi, ya bas yun hi, anjaane mein hua vyangya? Vyangya, jisne mujhe koi aur hi bana diya aur joh mujhe sai dhai teen saal badi hai. Jaise-jaise umar mein aage badhte hain, tareefon ke maayne bhi badalne lagte hain. Ab tareef seedhi nahin hoti, ya to kisi se tulna mein aati hai, ya phir aise-Lamhoon mein, "tum to pachaas ki lagti hi nahin!" jaise pachaas ki lagna koi gunaah ho.

"Tumhari aankhen Kajol jaisi hain,

Tumhari thodi Karishma jaisi hai,

Tumhari muskaan Madhubala jaisi hai,

Tum saari mein bilkul Sridevi lag rahi ho,

Tumhari body Hrithik jaisi hai,

Tumhari jawline Tiger Shroff jaisi hai,

Tum to bilkul Vicky Kaushal lag rahe ho!"

Haan, lekin agar thoda ageing ka tadka lag jaaye, to ye saare compliments ki tarah lagte hain."

Pata nahin, yeh pressure har generation mein tha ya hum zyada bawle ho rahe hain. Kuch keh nahin sakte. Vigyaan itni tarakki kar gaya hai, laser, tummy tuck, boob job, facelift, botox aur na jaane kya-kya. Kuch had tak, assi ka hone ke baad bhi, atharah ka dikhna sambhav ho gaya hai. Lekin kabhi socha hai, kya vichaaron ki surgery sambhav hai? Badalte waqt ke saath badalna kya zaroori hai? Kabhi apne aap se sawal bhi poochhe hain? Yahi sawaal ghere baitha tha mujhe ki rekha kahaan par kheenchhein? Par kya rekha kheenchhna itna aasan hai?

Yeh kashmakash hai, "Phir makeup hi kyun karein?", sirf saaf-suthre kapde pehnein aur andarooni roop ko baahari tvacha nikhaarne dein. Man to yahi kehta hai, aur phir aaina vichaar badal deta hai. Is udhedbun mein itna aage aa gaye hain ki ab ye sab namumkin prateet hota hai. Is tarazu mein to latke hi rehte hain aur har koi apne hisaab se ageing se joojhta nazar aata hai. Kya zamaana raha hoga bina aayeene ke, hum sirf doosron ko dekh sakte the, khud ko to sirf paani mein hi dekh sakte the, aur ab aaina, photo, social media, filter, fillers, zamaana hi alag hai.

"50 is the new 30" Kaash, "30 is the new 50" mein bhi wahi khushi hoti. Kya yeh behtar na hota ki 30, 30 hi rahe aur 50, 50 aur ismein bhi khushi chhipi hoti? Kahin kho rahe hain, par pata nahi kahaan aur kaise rokein? Kahin thahakon mein jhurrhiyon ka rudan chhupa lete hain shayad.

Mahabharat ka vah adhyay yaad aata hai, jahan Shri Krishna Karn se kehte hain, "Tumne sirf apne liye socha, samaj ke baare mein nahin socha, isliye tum paap ke bhaagidaar ho." Kya hum bhi bhaagidaar nahin ban rahe? Ageing ki side chupate-chupate, bahari sundarta par itna dhyan dete-dete, hum aane wali peedhi ki mansikta ko dhundhla kar rahe hain.

Par sach kahoon, toh ek samay ke baad shayad sulah ho hi jaati hai poori nahin, lekin thodi-thodi har din. Pehle jahan har ek line, har ek grey baal chubh jaata tha, ab wahi sab zyada disturb nahi karta. Ek din aise hi bina filter photo khinch jaati hai, aur hum use delete nahi karte. Ek din kisi party mein bina foundation ke chale jaate hain, aur wapas aake apne aap se khush bhi hote hain.

Waqt ke saath samajh aata hai ki self-worth ka chehra hota hi nahi hai, uski koi specific age, size ya glow nahi hota. Woh bas ek ehsaas hota hai ki main theek hoon, jaisi bhi hoon, main theek hoon ,Kuch toh izzat banti hai is body ki jisne taa-umar kumara saath diya, zindagi ke har utaar-chadhaav mein. Aur haan, kabhi kabhi fir bhi shak hota hai, par ab us shak se bhaagte nahi use chai ke saath baithkar samjha lete hain.

Kaash, ageing keval baahari sundarta tak seemit hoti, lagta hai, jhurrhiyaan haath se mastishk ki or safar kar rahi hain, lekin jhuriyaan haath se mastishk mein kaise?

Science mein to padha tha skull mein jhuriyaan nahi aati. Agar 20 saal ki Reshmi se poochhti, to main yahi kehti ki hargiz nahi, par 50 saal ki Reshmi ka vichaar aur anubhav alag hai. Lagta hai ageing, hamari soch, hamare drishtikon aur hamare faislon ko bhi prabhavit karti hai?

Bharat meri janmabhoomi hai aur Netherlands meri karmabhoomi. Hum har saal Bharat aate hain, rishtedaron se milna, hansi-mazaak, saath khaana, raat bhar gappein, kahin taash ka daur, kahin carrom ki gotiyan, kahin golgappe ki rehdi, to kahin doston sang Shimla-Ooty ki sair. Kuch isi tarah main ageing ki or aur aging mere or badh rahi thi. Shayad kuch desi nuskhe bhi iska hissa the, haldi, besan, aur thodi-si meethi yaadein.

Laga tha ki zindagi ek certain rhythm mein chal rahi hai, thoda nostalgia, thoda self-care, aur thodi desi mitti ki khushboo. Par umar ke saath yeh bhi samajh aane laga hai ki yeh rhythm kab badal jaaye kuch kaha nahi ja Saktey. Har saal ka aana–jaana, har mulaqat, har hansi ab thodi aur keemti lagne lagi thi, kyunki kahin na kahin andar se ehsaas hone laga tha ki waqt ab sirf aage nahi badh raha, kabhi-kabhi paas se bhi guzar raha hai. aisa isliye keh rahee hun kyunki kuch ghatneiyn aisee huee mere aas pass. Mere kareebe, jinhen kabhi sir dard nahin hua tha, halke sir dard ko lekar doctor ke paas gaye aur report mein nikla tumour. Socha, thodi koshish karte hain, jaan-pehchan ke doctor se salah lein. Doctor, jo khaasa dost bhi tha, phone par bola "Bharat aana hoga." Wahin, ek dost ki patni ka cancer ka ilaaj chal raha tha, aur isi beech ek aur dost ko stroke. Aur usi samay mere parichit ko autoimmune disorder, kaafi gambhir sthiti thi.

Ye kaisi jhurhiyan mehsoos kar rahi thi main? Ye jhurhiyan dekh nahin paa rahi thi, par mehsoos haath ki jhurhiyon se zyada kar rahi thi. Apno ko kho dene ka gham. Sach hai, ageing se kaafi seham jaati hoon main.

Ageing ka hi asar hai ki ab maa ko har teesre din phone kar leti hoon, behno se call, nanadon se to roz Snapchat. Sach kahoon, subah 6 baje sai pehle agar India ke number se call aa jaaye, to dil zara seham jaata hai. 2006 ki vah subah ki call, jiske baad sirf maa hi hamare paas hain. Aur sach kehti hoon, is lekh se pehle mujhe khud bhi nahi pata tha ki haath se mastishk ki or badhte jhurhiyoon se darti hoon mein.

Ab har waqt ka khul kar istemal karne lagi hoon, thoda apno mein seemit ho gayi hoon. Un logon ke saath zyada samay bitaati hoon, jin ke jaane ke baad ye afsos na ho ki kaash, unke saath pyara sa samay bitaaya hota. Sach hai, ageing ke saath kaafi seham jaati hoon.

Yeh ek chhota sa waaqya hai, lekin mere dil mein gehri jagah bana gaya. Haal hi mein main apni beti se baat kar rahi thi. Maine use bataya ki is baar main Bharat ek hafta pehle ja rahi hoon bas yun hi, maa ke saath thoda aur waqt bitaane ke liye. Bojhil awaaz mein kaha, "Thoda bodhi ho rahi hai maa."Kuch pal ki khamoshi ke baad, meri beti ne jo kaha, usne mujhe aur sochnein mein majboor kar diya.Usne bahut saadgi se kaha, "Mujhe accha laga ki aap aisa kar rahi ho. Aur aap sabmein se shayad Nani hi ise sabse zyada mehsoos karti hain umr ka asar, aur us samay ko jo har din chupchaap aage badhta jaa raha hai. Betiya ki baat ke baad thoda aur tezi se maa ke paas pahunchne ka mann hua. Jaise us ek pal ne yaad dila diya ho ki waqt sirf ghadi mein nahin, dil ke andar bhi chalta rehta hai.

Hum aksar bhool jaate hain ki jinse humne duniya dekahni shuru ki, wahi log ek din hamari duniya se chupchaap ojhal hone lagte hain. Aur tab sirf waqt nahi beetta, ek poori duniya beet jaati hai.

Shayad isiliye ab main zyada muskaraati hoon, maa ka haath thoda der tak thaame rakhti hoon, aur har baat ko ek aakhri baat ki tarah sunti hoon. Aap bhi sochiye kya kisi ke paas laut kar aane ka waqt hamesha rehta hai? Ya phir waqt hi to hai jo chupchaap beetta jaata hai...bina kahe, bina thahre. Is baar, maine thaharne ka faisla kiya.

Aur haan, ab toh ageing se dosti ho gayi hai. Pehle jahan anti-ageing creams ka budget grocery se zyada hota tha, ab lagta hai haldi-doodh aur maa ki daant hi kaafi hai. Kabhi socha tha ki ek din WhatsApp pai forward wali "Good morning" image bhi emotional kar degi? Aur Snapchat filters se zyada, maa ke saath li gayi ek halki si blurry photo zyada pyari lagti hai. Ab waqt ko rokna nahi chahti, bas uske saath ek cup chai zaroor peena chahti hoon. Aur agar kabhi koi keh de ki "Lagta hi nahi 50 ki ho!", toh muskuraakar kehti hoon "Lagta nahi, par pre menopause symptoms reminder de detai hain kabhi kabhi.

Haathon se fisalti rait,

Paani par tairti kagaz ki kashti,

Sardi mein silaiyon se nikle unke goley,

Aur garmi mein chhat par sukhti aam ki papdi.

Chhoti chhoti cheezein,

Jaise bachpan ki album se gira ek pal ho,

Phir se mil jaata hai kabhi mitti mein,

Kabhi kisi kahani ke beech se guzar kar.

Sab kuch waisa hi lagta hai

Bas, ab nani ke haathon ki jhurriyaan,

Mere haathon se mitti par kahaniyaan bunti hain.

Dil ab bhi

Baarish mein bheeg kar

Aasmaan se dosti kar leta hai.

Aur main…

Ek chai ki chuski ke saath,

Boondon ki thap mein

Apna hi kuch bhoola hua paa leti hoon.

Reshmi Nashier

❋ ❋ ❋

CHEHRE PAR WAQT KE NISHAN

Aaine mein pehli baar jab saamne ke do teen safed baal dekhe toh mann ko yeh keh kar bahla diya ki yeh toh nai nai shaadi ke baad sindoor lagane ke kaaran ya phir naye shahar mein badli hui hawa pani ke kaaran hue hai. Par aakhir kitni der tak koi insaan is sachhai se bhaag sakta hai ki har pal jo beet raha hai woh humein jeevan ke agle charan ke kareeb le ja raha hai. Jeevan ka har charan mahatvapurn hai, isliye jo insaan yahaan tak pahunch paaye woh bada hi khushkismat hai. Phir kyun aksar jab hum budhape ki baat karte hain to chinta, bhay aur udaasi ka ehsaas hota hai.

Aaina kabhi jhoot nahi bolta, par kya hum sach sunnay ke liye tayyar hote hain? Jab choti thi tab aksar ghanto aaine ke saamne baith apni muskaan, apni aankhein aur apni zulfon ko nihaarti thi. Lekin ab aaine se dar lagta hai. Ab jab aaine mein khud ko dekhti hoon to ek jaana pehchana par bahut hi alag, badla hua chehra nazar aata hai. Twacha par jhuriyaan aur baalon mein chandi jaise safedi jhalak ne lagi hai. "Main badhti umar se nahi darti" apne aap ko ye kehkar bahut samjhaane ki koshish karti hoon. Khud ko laakh samjhaane par bhi ki umar ka badhna ek prakritik prakriya hai, kabhi kabhi akele mein mann yeh soch kar udaas ho jaata hai ki main apne purane roop ki maatr parchhai hi reh gayi hoon.

Safed ke saath saath ab baal itne ghane bhi nahi rahe. Mujhe yaad hai jab pehle kanghi karte samay agar kuch baal ponytail se baahar reh jaate toh main unhein kheench kar tod deti thi. Ab jab main kanghi karti hoon toh haath me toote hue baalon ke guchhe khud hi aa jaate hain. Pehle jo chehre par chamak thi ab woh murjhane lagi hai. Aankhon ke neeche kale gaddhe padh gaye hain aur upar pe chashma.

Par agar khoobsurati sirf chehre ki hai toh kya vyaktitva ka koi mulye nahi? Uska koi aakarshan nahi?

Kabhi kabhi sochti hoon ki, is badhti umar ka ehsaas kab hua. Us din jab raasta puchne ke liye maine car roki tub us ladke ne kaha ki "aunty" aap aage se right le lena ya jab dosto ne "badi sundar lag rahi ho" ki jagah "apni umar ke liye badi acchi lag rahi ho" kehna shuru kiya. Ya jab kuch bhi khane ya na khane par bhi wajan bus badhta hi chale jaye jaise koi lambi daud mein laga ho aur kum hone ka naam hi na le, ya phir jab pati dev ke mooh se nikal jaaye ki "kahi yeh rang kuch zyada bright toh nahi hai".

Aksar jab main budhape ke baare mein sochti hoon toh yeh parivartan mujhe kaafi chunautipurn lagta hai. Aur kyun na ho? Apne maa baap ko jinko hamesha pathar ki deewar ke jaise mere saath khade dekha tha ab woh utne mazboot nahi nazar aate. Ab us deewar mein daraarein nazar aati hain. Kai bimariyon ne ab apna ghar bana liya hai. Unhe is asahay haal mein dekhkar aksar apne bhavishya ki pratibimb nazar aati hai. Doosra dar jo budhapa saath lekar aata hai woh hai akelepan ka dar. Umar ke saath saath har koi apni zindagi mein vyast ho jaata hai jisse dost bhi kum ho jaate hain. Kuch dost dusre desh ya shahar toh kuch doosri duniya hi chale jaate hain. Bachhe bhi apne ghar parivar aur career mein vyast ho jaate hain aur unke paas bhi itna samay nahi hota.

Race ki shuruaat mein dhaavak ki nazar raaste par hoti hai. Jaise jaise woh aage badhta hai tab raasta chhota hone lagta hai yahaan tak ki jab lagbhag aadha raasta paar ho jaye toh use phir manzil saaf nazar aane lagti hai. Shuruat mein kabhi bhi ant nazar nahi aata jab ki pata hota hai ki manzil wohi hai. Har ek pal humein usi ki oar kareeb le ja raha hota hai.

Jab ek bachha bada ho raha hota hai tab uske maa baap se lekar parivar aur samaaj ke sab log uski madad karte hain ki woh bada hokar ek khushaal zindagi ji sakein. Hum uski saari ichhayein aur zaruraton ko poora karte hain. Hum shuruaat mein toh hamesha madad ke liye tayyar hote hain, par kya humne budhape ke liye apne aap ko tayyar kiya hai? Jabki humein pata hota hai ki budhapa is jeevan yatra ka woh abhin ang hai jo janm ke samay hi shuru ho jaata hai. Par hum shaayad dar ke kaaran is haqeeqat se muh modh lete hain aur jab zindagi ke is charan par pahunchte hain toh apne aap ko ekdum bebas aur lachar paate hain. Jeevan ke shuruat mein jahan hum logon ki bheed se ghiray hote hain, ant mein wahan, sirf sannata sath reh jaata hai. Par vijeta wahi hai jisne sannate ke liye taiyari ki ho. Tayari hi humein utsav ki aur le jaati hai. Jab hum shuruaat ki itni sundar tayari karte hain toh phir ant ki kyun nahi?

Budhapa kab shuru hota hai iska uttar sabke liye alag hota hai. Haan, beshak mere sharir ne jeevan ke is purnata ko sweekar kar liya ho par mann uske saath nahi chalta. Mann abhi bhi wahi hai jahan saalon pehle tha. Umango se bhara aur sapno se saja. Aaj bhi jab main purane gaane sunti hoon ya doston ke saath masti karti hoon ya apne bachon ke saath hasti aur baatein karti hoon toh masti aur zindadili pehle jaise hi hoti hai. Sharir beshak boodha ho jaaye par mann hamesha jawan hi rehta hai. Iska ehsaas mujhe meri 86 saal boodhi maa ne karaya. Aksar woh kanghi karte samay poochti hai ki unke baal itne kyu jhad rahe hain ya phir bade aashcharya se apne haathon ki jhurriyon ko dekhkar ye poochti hai ki unke haath ki nasein kyun nazar aa rahi hain. Unke is prashna se yeh khyaal aata hai ki shaayad umar ka budhape se kuch lena dena nahi hai. Umar sirf ek sankhya hai, asli jawani toh mann aur soch mein hoti hai. Aur jab tak mann jawan hai, zindagi har roz nayi lagti hai.

Maana ki budhapa jeevan ki yatra ka woh abhin ang hai jo praay har khushnaseeb insaan ko tay karna padta hai. Yeh sirf khone ka naam nahi hai jahan yaaddash, jawani, dost aur swasthya sab khone ka khauf mann mein gathan karta hai, naahi jhukte kandhon ka samay, balki unche anubhav ka samay hai. Aise anubhav jo doosron ka jeevan sanwaar sakte hain. Yahaan har ek jhurri ek dastaan bayan karti hain aur har safed baal ek anubhav. Yahaan tak pahuchhte pahuchhte maine bahut kuch paaya hai. Har pal ne mujhe kuch na kuch diya hi hai, chahe woh kisi apne ka saath ho ya kisi apne ke jaane ka dard. Aur yeh bhi samajh aaya hai ki jeevan sirf safaltaon ka yogfal nahi, balki un anubhavon ka sangrah hai jisne mujhe insaan banaya hai. Main abhari hu in saare palon ke liye, jo mujhe bana gaye, aur un logon ke liye jo mere safar mein saath rahe. Budhapa sachmuch ek aisi kavita hai jise waqt anubhav ki siyahi se likhta hai.

Aaj mujhe apne mata pita ke liye wahi majboot deewar banne ka mauka mila hai. Apne badhte umar ke saath, yeh ek vishesh anubhav hai. Apne maa-baap ko pyaar aur himmat se sambhalna, unke liye ek sahara ban paana, jaise wo kabhi mere liye the. Jivan ki saanjh har pal ek nayi zimmedari aur pyaar ke rang ko saath laati hai. Ye mere rishte ko aur gehra banati hai.

Mera ye vishwas ki jo dekhbhal, baatein aur seekh maine apne bachho ko di hai, usne ek aisi peedhi ko saksham banaya hai jo is duniya ko ek behtar jagah bana sakte hain. Yeh anubhav aur aatmavishwas meri andaruni khoobsurati ka hissa hai. Aur yeh sada mehekte rahenge basant ki pehli hawa ki tarah.

Mujhe aaj bhi woh shaam bade achhe se yaad hai jab main apni balcony me khadi, suraj ko dheere dheere samundar ki gehraiyon mein samaate hue dekh rahi thi. Aakash kesariya rang mein ranga hua tha. Thandi hawa mere chehre ko halke se chhoo kar jaise mujhse kuch keh rahi thi. Mujhe yeh ehsaas hua ki, jaise har din suraj doob kar naye subah ki tayari karta hai, waise hi zindagi bhi har pal naye roop mein ubharti hai.

Ab jab main aaine mein khud ko dekhti hoon toh dar nahi lagta. Ek halki si muskurahat chehre par aa jaati hai kyunki jo chehra aaj aaine mein dikhta hai usme sirf umar nahi, ek kahani hai. Aankhon ke koney, jo kabhi sirf muskurahat ki rekhaon se saja karte the, aaj un me gehraeyi hai, anubhav hai. Ek ajeeb si swatantrata hai mujhe, doosron ko prabhavit karne ki chinta kam aur apne asli swaroop ke saath jeene ka saahas. Main ab sampann hoon. Anubhavon se, samvedana se, aur apne hone ki poornata se. Main pehle ki tarah khoobsurat nahi balki pehle se bhi zyada khoobsurat hoon kyunki ab mere paas mere anubhav, meri samajhdari aur meri atma ki sundarta hai..... kyunki ab main sirf dikhayi nahi, mehsoos bhi hoti hoon.

Satya Akhouri

✳ ✳ ✳

Food

खानपान

LIKE AN EPIPHANY OF LOVE
AND AN UNBREAKABLE BOND WITH HOME

Food is love, memory, and an unspoken language passed down through generations. It is the thekua cradled in a father's palm at the airport, the treasured recipes a grandmother never revealed, and the quiet comfort of a mother's kitchen, where flavors were not just cooked but told as stories. It is the mischievous laughter of siblings stealing powdered milk, the playful deceit of swapping tinda for guava, and the silent affection in a husband's smile over a meal imperfectly made but deeply felt.

It is the scent of festival sweets that lingers long after the celebrations, the warmth of chai prepared just right, and the echo of grandmothers' hands kneading love into every meal. It is in fathers who would cross cities to taste something extraordinary, in mothers who carried tradition even when they never embraced the kitchen, and in the midnight, kheer stolen from the fridge, each bite a whisper of the past.

Between tradition and change, between the aroma of childhood and the flavors of the future, we realize food is more than what we eat. It is the bridge that connects generations, the warmth of home that lingers across distances, and the simplest way love finds its voice.

MY TALES OF FOOD AND MORE

I was born in the city of Calcutta, and my early years were steeped in the rich culture and timeless traditions of Bengal. The first decade of my life unfolded amidst the chaos and warm embraces of this metropolis, in a typical yet not-so-typical middle-class Bengali family, each moment etching indelible marks upon the canvas of my being. Those ten years laid the foundation for the values I hold dear today, shaping the person I would become as an adult.

During the years in Kolkata, the influence of my paternal and maternal families, who were at the two ends of the Bengali culture spectrum, had a lasting influence on me – a realization I had decades later, far, far away from the city of my birth.

The gastronomy of my paternal and maternal families, the art and expertise involved in preparing and eating food epitomized their distinct characteristics and was a true reflection of their very being.

My paternal home in South Calcutta, where I was born and lived till the age of ten, was a big red and white corner house on Rash Behari Avenue, a bustling street of the metropolis. A street known for housing many of the city's old families, with famed sweet shops, each known for their unique specialities. It is often said this area was developed primarily by a generation of English-educated professionals, like lawyers, college teachers, and medical practitioners, who came with a new fashion: a mix of literary and musical traditions, along with the Western social values. I always found the house rather odd and could never understand what exactly the architect had in mind when planning it. I had heard from my parents that because of the various extensions and partitions to the original edifice over the years, it had somehow lost its old glory.

The kitchen was housed on the ground floor, and it consisted of three interconnected rooms. This is where my grandmother, along with her cook of some twenty years and a couple of other helpers, could be found conjuring up the elaborate Bengali meals every day. Our family house, or bari, as it was generally referred to in Kolkata, and my grandmother in particular, was famed for their expertise in traditional Bengali cuisine. In fact, she was apparently so good that my parents' friends, if they came for a visit closer to a mealtime, would get themselves forcibly invited to have a meal.

Thamma (my paternal grandmother) guarded her recipes very closely and never shared them with anyone. I remember when we were about to relocate to Delhi, Ma asked her repeatedly for the recipes of some of her specialities and she, smiling wryly, would say, 'Oi tel Nun, holud' – just oil, salt, and haldi. Chakradhar, our famed Odia cook, was probably the only one who knew the secrets because his cooking was no less perfect, and, at times, I have heard people say maybe even a notch better. If Thamma was the gastronome, my grandfather was the ultimate connoisseur, and I am sure it was to his benefit she guarded her expert knowledge lest she lose the power she had on her ever-adoring husband. However, in my growing up days, Thamma was, in reality, just the head chef and Chakradhar the sous chef. She cooked only on very special occasions, and that was limited to one or two things. My grandfather, the ultimate patriarch, was a connoisseur par excellence, but strictly for Bengali food. He just didn't recognize any other cuisine and was terribly offended each time my parents went out for meals. He loved to eat and feed others around him; to him, the mere act of eating was a celebration of sorts. Feasts were a thing to reckon with in our house.

The fish had to be cut to the right size, the vegetables fresh and cooked with the appropriate level of spice, the accompanying seasonal chutneys made of mango, gooseberry, and pineapple to finish off the heavy meal. The right variety of rice – I recall sacks of different types of rice grains stacked up in the pantry. For me, it was difficult to distinguish one from the other, but he could spot with a morsel if the right variety was used. There was basmati for biryani, gobindo bhog for khichuri and payesh. And many other local Bengal varieties, some of which maybe are even lost now in the mainstream. My mother, in her kitchen, used only one variety, and so do I.

The tea-time savouries nimki, samosa, and luchi had to be always accompanied by the most suitable complementing sweets. The sweets were sourced from the specialty shops of my grandfather's choice. Even on a regular day, there could be no compromise, and if there was a failing, the staff had a tough time. I often wondered as a child how come a person so qualified, erudite, a brilliant lawyer could be so concerned about food, the mere act of eating, and demand such a level of excellence. Little did I realize it was truly the reflection of the person he was, and probably that was why Thamma never shared the recipes.

As long as my parents were alive, decades after we had left Kolkata, there were regular references to the culinary excellence of our home left behind. At times, Ma used to try her hand at replicating some of the complicated recipes of my grandmother. Probably she had sneakily acquired the recipes from the cook, and after trying it out, Bapi would always say, 'Thik ma r moto noye' – 'Not exactly like Ma's'. I wish I had tried getting the recipes from Thamma; maybe I would have been luckier. I'm not sure if there is anyone left carrying on her legacy. If only she had the prudence to teach her skills to the gen next instead of holding on to the knowledge she thought gave her a power over others. She completely overlooked the fact that our respect and love for her was beyond her culinary prowess.

My mother's side of the family was a stark contrast to my paternal home. They had long moved out of their ancestral house in Lansdowne around the late 1960s to a beautiful modern villa in an upcoming South Kolkata neighbourhood. It housed my maternal grandfather, his two younger brothers, and their wives – my three favourite grandmothers, each unique in their own way. The children by then had all been married and left home. This was a household steeped in Brahmo culture, and it had a very liberal Westernized lifestyle. It was much later in life when I realized that the ease with which I moved in and out of these two contrasting households laid the foundations of the person I am today.

Most of the empty wall spaces in my paternal home were taken up by pictures and sculptures of deities, whereas in my maternal home, I had never seen a single picture of any deity or any object remotely connected to any religion. There was no puja room or any compulsory prasad on Thursday after Lakshmi Puja or fasting on an auspicious day. To me, it was natural, and the two harmoniously co-existed in me. It seemed very natural to me that my maternal grand-aunts and grandmothers never adorned themselves with a Hindu marriage symbol, like sindur, bindi, or the noa (bangle), whereas in my father's house, it was unthinkable for a married woman to be without it.

In spite of their many differences, the one thing these families had in common was their love for gastronomy and their par-excellence culinary expertise.

Mamarbari, (my maternal grandparent's house) for me, was an absolute treat in every possible way. Not a big lover of traditional Bengali cuisine,

I enjoyed the food there and so looked forward to our weekend visits, which were an absolute feast. Each grandma tried to outdo the other. My favourite was Chordida (youngest grandma); her speciality was continental food, and she was amazing. Her variety of sandwiches, devilled eggs, baked Bhetki with a crusty breadcrumb coating, spinach balls with shrimp fillings, omelette with a light filling of minced meat and cheese, a variety of soups... the list goes on. She had learnt from the best, especially during her travels to the west. Cooking was her passion, and she took it to an all-new level. Ma and her cousins would be constantly asking Chordida for her latest recipes during our weekend meals or asking her advice as to why their experiments in the kitchen failed. She would be constantly handing out handwritten recipes and advising the girls how to make their lives easier in the kitchen. She was especially mindful of the sons-in-law and knew each one's favourite. Bapi and Chordida had a very special relation. In all seriousness, many a time he had asked her to publish her recipe book, but she would laugh it off and tease him instead that it was a hint she should make something special for him.

My dida,(maternal grandmother) the eldest of the three, was excellent in Indian cuisines, not just Bengali. Her specialities were southern Indian cuisines, Mughlai, and dishes from North India and Bengal, of course. Not to mention the perfection with which she could make the complicated Bengali sweets. This was all thanks to her friends from different communities and finally moving out of Kolkata to make Bangalore in South India home.

She was one hell of a socializer, and in today's world could have easily qualified as a micro influencer. She was the most beautiful of the three, always immaculately dressed but true to Brahmo traditions, never making any show of opulence, no garish jewellery but everything subtle and simple.

The grandfathers were no less gastronomes. Though hopeless in the kitchen, they were famed for their ability to scout places in Kolkata and its outskirts for specialities. They could travel for hours just to try out one dish at a remote village. I recall one incident, travelling to Raniganj by car to eat mutton curry and rice in the town's railway station waiting room. Apparently, it was unique. I, of course, have no recollection how it tasted.

Both the families were famed for their elaborate lunches and dinners. Each feast, no matter how small, was planned to perfection. In retrospect, I feel they expressed their values and emotions through food. One held on to the traditions of the past, the other developed a new modern liberal world, but both respected the other.

Once we relocated to Delhi and started life in a nuclear family, my relation with food changed. Ma was a good cook but pragmatic, and in the midst of household chores, without the entourage of helpers and cooks as it was back in Kolkata, she preferred to keep it simple and healthy. She did not believe in the kitchen paraphernalia. However, both she and Bapi loved eating out. Our neighbourhood in Delhi boasted some great eateries, and very soon, my parents had their list of favourite joints. Of course, they were nostalgic about Kolkata Nizam's kathi rolls and the perfect cocktail sausages and cold cuts, which, according to them, were non-existent in Delhi.

In our house in GK, regular meals were predictable – nothing over the top. Of course, when my parents entertained, Ma did manage to put up quite a spread with the help of a hired cook or the many caterers around. Again, there was the obsession for perfection, size, quality, and quantity, something she definitely inherited from her parents and in-laws.

Ma, an introvert by nature and completely disinterested in housework, never really bothered to brush up her culinary skills or add to her repertoire. To her, time spent in the kitchen was a complete waste, so she was more than happy to denounce it while Dida would be visiting us in Delhi. Each time Dida would come to visit us, she would stay for three to six months. Ma was never seen near the kitchen, and it was feast time. As usual, she would come armed with a million new recipes. Once dida passed away and Ma slowly aged, we had a cook coming daily to take care of our meals.

I was out of the house in university, and when I came home on vacation, I had to endure the most despicable food ever. At times, Ma would still cook a few things, but it was rare. As I reminisced about the grandeur of my grandmother's cooking, I often wondered how come Ma never learnt dida's famous recipes, barring just a few. This remained a mystery to me always, and much later in life, I realized it was a result of who Ma was; household chores, cooking, or even the art of homemaking were never for her. Her dreams were different and her expectations from life were many. Probably Bapi was the only one who understood that. He also realized it was beyond him to fulfil her dreams. His love for her was boundless, and hence, he quietly accepted Ma's indifference to the mundane chores of everyday life. From time to time, he would casually refer to the homemade delicacies he so missed, but somewhat it was as if never audible to Ma.

My relation with food was way less complicated, and it changed with the various phases of life. As a student staying in a hostel to being away from home and country, it was all about convenience. Moreover, I was very comfortable with continental cuisine and never really pined for Indian or home-cooked food. It was about getting a hearty meal with the least effort because I loved eating. I could never really understand some of the other Indian students in our university who would carry exotic spices diligently back from India after every vacation and spend a considerable part of their free time looking for Indian veggies, goat meat, or other paraphernalia to drum up an Indian meal which would finally turn out nowhere even close to the authentic dishes back home. I would have my fill of Indian meals when I travelled back to Delhi during holidays. While at university, I preferred to experience international traditions, mainly European and local Russian cuisines. It opened a whole new culinary world to me, a world that was completely unknown. My relation to food at this stage of my life was reflective of my general mindset those days. I was discovering new places, cultures, experiences, relationships, and friends. Having left India and living as a student, I wanted to envelop the whole world as much as possible within those five or six years. I was not sure, after the completion of my studies, if I would again come back to Europe. India was home and would always be there. Little did I know it was destined to be very different.

Fast-forward three decades. I am still in Europe, I am now a citizen of the Netherlands, a country that cannot really pride itself on culinary excellence. I am a wife, a mother – yes, a lot has happened in these years, and in some ways, my relation to food has also changed, for better and for worse. I never formally learnt cooking; I simply picked it up on the way. I could never follow a recipe to the dot as I felt it then lacked originality – whenever I cooked or had to cook, I would tweak the recipe and alter it to my taste and mood. Probably that was one of the reasons I never could replicate the famous delicacies of our home back in Kolkata: it required discipline, practise, and rigid observance of every minute detail. I was too much of a liberal in mind and body to be restricted within the lines. I cooked well – it was palatable and sometimes even good – but it was never the classic, instead, a medley of many tastes. I had my own interpretations of the many famed dishes from my grandparents' home, and though they were not authentic, they were unique in their own way. My husband, Vikas, is a food critic and, as destiny would have it, a very good cook, with the right instincts and taste buds of a chef. He does not particularly like the Bengali cuisine, but he absolutely loves a few of my creations which I passed off as Bengali but knew were far from the original. Then again, cooking is creative. Why should we have to adhere to that one recipe and try replicating the same?

In our home in Amsterdam, food is simple but carefully planned and tastefully prepared. My dida's golden rule still echoes: you need patience and the best quality ingredients to make the perfect dish. Vikas, too, believes in it, and we try to avoid shortcuts and prepare our daily meals and those when entertaining with care and love! Many Western dishes have become a part of our daily cuisine, just as many Western habits are a part of our everyday life.

Food still remains a quintessential part of life, and it continues to be a great source of pleasure and satisfaction. But I see with time the act of eating is losing its importance – the cacophony around health and food, the rights and wrongs, the must eat and never eat is at times overbearing, robbing us of the simple undiluted pleasure of just eating. The simple pleasure of reminiscing the yesteryears, or a life that has passed or some forgotten moments by simply preparing a dish.

As I had mentioned earlier, my gastronomy and its evolution, in a strange way, has reflected me, the person I am at various stages of life, and I have observed the same in the humans in my close vicinity. It will continue to be the most reliable yardstick in this rather unsettling world for me to judge who exactly you are!

Sharing one of my favourite recipe with a special twist from my dida, elevating it to a sublime level though a traditional Bengali cook will probably not accept this as authentic.

Teel Mach (Rahu/Carp in Mustard Oil)

Ingredients:

8–10 pieces of fresh Rahu or Carp, cut into medium-sized pieces (not too thin)

1 teaspoon turmeric powder

1 teaspoon red chili powder

Salt to taste

1 teaspoon nigella seeds (kalonji)

1 large tomato, grated smoothly (do not blend)

2 + 1½ tablespoons mustard oil (for cooking + finishing)

A few slit green chilies (for aroma and heat)

Method:

Prep the Fish: Sprinkle the fish l with turmeric and salt, mix well. Lightly fry the fish in mustard oil (or any preferred oil) until golden. Set aside.

Infuse the Oil: In a wok, heat 2 tablespoons of mustard oil until it just starts to smoke. Add the nigella seeds and let them crackle, but be careful not to burn them.

Prepare the Spice Mix: In a bowl, mix turmeric, red chili powder, salt, and a glass of water. Stir well to ensure there are no lumps.

Cook the Base: Carefully pour the spice mixture into the hot oil and let it simmer for about 2 minutes until the raw aroma of turmeric dissipates.

Add the Tomato(this was dida's twist): Stir in the grated tomato and let the mixture cook for a minute, allowing the flavors to meld.

Introduce the Fish: Gently place the fried fish into the simmering gravy. Let it cook for 5–8 minutes until the gravy thickens slightly and the oil starts to float to the surface.

Final Touch: Add a few slit green chilies for a burst of flavor. Just before turning off the heat, drizzle 1½ tablespoons of raw mustard oil over the gravy—this is what gives the dish its signature depth and aroma.

Serve & Enjoy: Best enjoyed hot with steaming rice, as the mustard oil lingers on your palate, bringing back memories of home.

P.S. This was a staple at home while growing up but due to some explicable reason I did not bother to acquaint myself with the recipe. First dida and then ma, they were there to make it. A few months before ma passed away, I had casually asked her for the recipe!

Shayonti Chatterji

❋ ❋ ❋

❋ ❋ ❋

Some stories don't start with "Once upon a time," but with the sound of mustard seeds popping or the smell of ghee on a warm paratha.The last piece was in English, this one hums the same tune in Hindi, written in Roman script, just like the way we share recipes or food memories when we miss home. Because food isn't just about taste, it's maa ke haath ka khana, school ka dabba, ek cup chai ka sukoon.

Chalo, khane ki baat karte hain... aur aap se apne khane ki yaadein, ehsaas, aur kahaniyan baant te hain.

❋ ❋ ❋

AANKH MICHOLI - KHANA AUR EHSAASON KI

Kabhi maa ke haath ke parathon mein, to kabhi adhpake ehsaason mein.

Jazbaaton ki talaash mein, kabhi chatpate thahakon mein.

Kabhi mithai mein ghuli puraani hansi mein.

Khana kuch khaas hai,

Khataas mein, mithaas mein, shraddha mein, bhakti mein,

Umang mein, tripti mein, chatpati hansi mein, namkeen aansoo mein,

Holi ki masti mein, Diwali ki roshni mein.

Khana kaafi khaas hai,

Nani ki god mein, maa ki mamta mein,

Bhai-behan ki nok jhok mein, doston ki hansi mein,

Nayi naveli ki sharam mein, navjat shishu ki ghutti mein,

Yoddha ke tilak mein.

Khana waaqai khaas hai,

Tapakti hui chutney mein, paan ki peek mein,

Chai ki chuski mein, aankhon ke rudan mein,

Prarthana ke bhog mein, Shabri ke ber mein.

Khana sach mein khaas hai.

Maine kaha tha apni introduction mein, agar aap mere se vartalap karte... khane ke baare mein kuch bhi likhna mere liye kisi vartalap se kam nahin aur yahi wajah hai ki yeh lekh bhi kuch vartalap jaisa hai.

Yaadon ka samundar umad kar aa raha hai, aur bahut saare ehsaason mein doob rahi hoon...Aaj jis jagah par hoon (49 years with few more months to be 50, an empty nester) Wahan sabse zyada pyaar shayad pati se hi hai, Shayad isiliye yaadon ka safar wahin se shuru hota hai. Mere aur mere pati ke rishte ki buniyad bhi khana hi hai. Hamari shaadi ke shuruaati din, ek saath rasoi mein bitaaye wo pal, Beshkeemti the, jahan bas pyaar ka swaad ghula tha. Do log aur das-baarah rotiyan, paanch logon ke barabar sabzi-daal. Phir bhi pet se zyada dil bharta tha. Sirf main jaanti hoon wo ehsaas, jab Anil, mere pati, muskura kar kehte "Tum aloo paratha sabse acche banati ho."Us pal, main das-baarah aasmaan upar hoti!

Kaafi haseen shuruaat thi hamari, Jismein khane ka yogdaan kaafi had tak amoolya raha hai.

Shuruaat ke pal Noida mein, chauthi manzil par, har Shukravaar ko anda bhurji aur khoob saare paranthe khaye humne. Pati slab par baithe rehte the, hum saath saath hi khana banate the. Un lamhon mein kuch jadugari ho gayi. Tab ye shabd nahi the, "soulmate", Bas itna tha ki hum ikatthe khana banate, ikatthe baith kar khate. Na mehngi thaali, na mehngi chamach, Na koi dining table, na koi kursi, zameen par baithte the, aur jis bartan mein khana pakaya usi se khate the. Aur kuch gazab hua! Wo rishta kuch aisa juda us khane se, ki aageaane wale sare utaar-chadhaav, Hamara pyaar bhara rishta jhel gaya.

25 saal ho gaye hain shaadi ko, phir bhi hum ek saath khana banate hain, Grocery bhi ek saath karte hain, aur in kaamon ki jadugari, bade se bade jhagde ko bhi chhota kar deti hai. Kaha tha na, khane ki baat nikli hai, Kai saari yaadon ka pitara khulega.

Arey!! Aap kahan kho gaye...Shayad kisi apne ke saath guzare rasoi ke lamhon mein. "Khane ki yahi khaasiyat hai ye sirf pet nahi bharta, ye dilon ko jodta hai. Sach mein, khana kuch khaas hai!"

Zindagi ke safar mein rishton ki prathamiktaayein badalti rehti hain, par shayad bachche hamesha partner se pehle nahin to immediate baad mein aate hain. Khane ka mahatva mujhe tab samajh mein aaya jab meri bitiya ne mere pati se khaana banana sikha. Tab khaana sirf swaad nahin raha, balki rishte ka ek gehra rang ban gaya. Sach mein, khaana kuch khaas hai!

Us samay main apne bete ke saath Bharat mein thi, uski cricket training ke liye. Yeh sunne mein shayad ajeeb lage, lekin usse pehle main aur meri bitiya, mere pati aur bitiya ke muqable zyada qareeb the, shayad thoda sa hi sahi, par farq tha. Phir cooking classes shuru hui, aur na jaane kaise, mere pati aur bitiya ke beech ka rishta ek nai gehraayi tak pahunch gaya. Jitni nikatata mere aur meri bitiya ke beech thi, ve dono usse ek kadam aage nikal gaye. Dekhiye na, khaana jaadu kar gaya!

Ab meri bitiya jaise khaana banati hai, kaash main bhi waisa kar paati! Saath ke saath safai, saath ke saath saara kaam, sab kuch itna sahaj aur khoobsurti se. Yeh sab usne mere pati se seekha. Sach mein, khaana sirf swaad nahin, yeh bahut kuch sanjota hai.

Main do bachchon ki maa hoon, betiya job mein, aur beta college mein, par dono ghar se door. Dono hi bachchon ki pasand bahut alag hai. Jab bhi in dono mein se koi ghar aata hai, to poori grocery list badal jaati hai, aisa lagta hai jaise koi tyohaar ho raha ho! Khoob khushi hoti hai, bade dil se, chaav se, wo sab banati hoon jo unhein pasand hai. Mere khayal se hum sabhi ki yahi kahani hai. Sach mein, khaana kuch khaas hai.

Khaane ki khaasiyat isse bhi aage jaati hai. Meri bitiya aur main aksar parties mein chupke se thoda samay nikal kar ek doosre ko ek nivaala khilate hain. Us pal mein itna pyaar bhara hota hai ki sach mein khaana khaas ban jata hai.

Mera beta bhi kuch kam nahin, kabhi-kabhi wo bhi mere liye chai banata hai, specially jab halka sa sir dard ho, kitni khushi milti hai us ek cup mein. Kabhi-kabhi brag bhi karti hoon is baat ko doston ke saath, ki dekho, usne bina kahe samjha aur chai mein sirf adrak nahin, thoda sa pyaar bhi daala. Choti-choti baaton mein jab apnapan chalakta hai, to lagta hai, zindagi bas inhi lamhon ka naam hai. Aur kya wo sirf ek chai hoti hai? Nahin! Wo chai nahin, us mein ghuli parwah, apnapan, aur sneh khaas hota hai. Shayad mera sir dard chai se theek hota hai, ya shayad us dekhbhal se, jo chai ke har ghoont mein basi hoti hai. Kamaal hai na, khane ki jadugari!

Khaane ki jadugari hi to hai ki aaj bhi nani ki yaad khaane se shuru hoti hai. Unki chhavi chulhe ke sameep baithi, aloo ki sabzi banati hui hi dikhti hai. Aloo ki sabzi, nooni ghee, bohiye mein rakhi roti, aaj bhi aisa ehsaas hota hai ki nani mere saath hi to hain. Nani to nahin, par shukr hai bhagwan ka ki Maa ke haath ka khaana yaadon mein jakar dhoondhna nahin padta. Meri maa shaakahari hain, par roasted chicken sabse badhiya banati hain.

Aaj bhi kai baar farmaish kar chuki hoon roasted chicken ki, par papa ke chale jaane ke baad yaad nahi, kab maa ne mere liye roasted chicken banaya ho. Churma zaroor banati hain, mera pasandida hai. Sach hai, ek hi pal mein khaana kisi ko pyaar karne aur kisi ko yaad karne ka tarika ban jata hai.

Ab to khaane ke kisse ghar mein ghus gaye, to bhai-behan ki baat na ho? Unse pitna hai... unki plate se cheez churaana, phir pakde jana, phir bina wajah hansi aana, aur maa ki daant se pehle ek-doosre ko bacha lena, kya din the wo bhi...Chalo, wahi kisse chhedte hain. Ek natkhat sa kissa meri behno ke saath. Hum sab bahut shauk se powder milk khate the. Ek din humne tay kiya, humne kya, meri badi behnon ne tay kiya,ki aaj kasam khate hain ki powder milk nahin khayenge. Mummy ko dikkat hoti hai jab kuch banana hota hai. Phir tay hua, kasam kaun khayega? Sabse pehle number chhote ka hi aaya. Lo, maine kasam khali "Aaj ke baad powder milk nahin khayenge!"Aur phir kya tha, dono bol uthi "Hum kasam nahin khayengi!" Chalo, ek ummedvaar kam hua powder milk ka. Hum behnon ki umr mein zyada farq nahin hai, Sabita ek saal badi hai, Sumita teen saal, aur Punita di chaar saal. Shayad umr ke farq aur swabhaav ke kaaran, badi behan is kisse ka hissa nahin thi.

Us samay to bhaav yaad nahin, par phir bhi aaj is kisse ko kai baar dohraate hain. Khoob hanste hain, aur wo kissa hamari har mehfil ka ek atoot waaqya ban gaya hai. Kuch in natkhat palon mein hum behnein dost ban gayi. Kamaal karta hai ye khaana bhi!

Bhai bhi kaafi pyaara hai humein, Khaane ki baat ho aur uska zikr na ho... aisa kaise ho sakta hai? Aisa kehte hain log ki main khaana theek hi bana leti hoon, par iski shuruaat bhai ke saath hui thi. Bhai bhi accha khana banaate hain. Ab tak yaad hai, ek raat ko chupke se rasoi mein humne shahi tamatar banaye. Chupke se isliye ki agar shor hua, to maa-baap se daant milegi. Par bahut badhiya shahi tamatar bane. Aaj bhai hotel industry mein hain, Norwegian Cruise Line mein General Manager hain. Kisko pata tha ki ye khaane ka shauk, khaana banane ka shauk, hospitality industry mein le jaayega bhai ko!

Sabse badi didi ke bhi kai kisse hain, Sabse latest wala share karti hoon aapse. Abhi humne apni pachaasvi salgirah manayi poori shaadi dobara, aisa samajh lo. Aur meri badi behan Punita di ne, jitne bhi mehmaan aaye, unke liye khud se laddoo banaye. Aadha kilo ke laddoo, har mehmaan ke liye! Kariban 80 mehmaan to honge. Itni mehnat, itna pyaar! Sach mein, khaana kuch khaas hai.

Behno ke saath jijaji to package deal hain. Hamare jijaji, jo shayad hamare liye, hamare papa ki jagah par hain. Ye pehli baar humne, thodi saali hone ke kaaran, thodi choti hone ke kaaran, hum teenon behno ne shararat kari. Amrood ki jagah, tinda katkar, namak, cheeni, neembu lagakar khaane ko de diya. Jijaji bhi army ke hain. To jo unhone halke se humko daant lagaayi, teenon behno ko, hamare aansuon ki dhaar bah nikli! Phir kya tha, jijaji samajh gaye ki shararat kar rahi hain, par itni shararti hain nahin! Uske baad ice cream khane gaye the hum, aur uske baad jijaji se rishta thoda alag ho gaya. Thoda zyada pyaar bhara aur izzat bhara ho gaya. Kamaal kar jaata hai ye khana bhi! Kehne ko to tinda hi tha, par yaadein de gaya.

Sirf rishte hi nahin, sabziyaan bhi kisi kisse ki yaad dila deti hain. Lo, tinde se bhi ek yaad aayi. Ek baar papa ki posting Jhunjhunu mein thi, wahan bahut tinda banta tha khaane mein. Tinde humein katai pasand nahin the. Ek chammach tinde ki sabzi ke saath aadha glaspaani pee jaate the. Majaal ki hum bolein, "Humein nahin khaana hai!" Wo time wahi tha, jo khaana bana hai, sab wahi khaayenge, sab ek saath baithenge. Tab khaana wahin tha. Aaj, kabhi-kabhi dekhti hoon, sochti hoon, agar ghar mein chaar bachche hain, chaaron ki farmaishon ka khaana banta hai. Thoda daur badla, khana badalte daur ki buniyaad sa hi lagta hai.

Chalo, khaane ke is safar mein thoda ghar se baahar chalte hain Agar aap ka janm varsh 1970 se 1985 ke beech ka hai Aur agar aapne Kendriya Vidyalaya se padhai ki hai to aap zaroor meri agli yaad se jud jaaoge. Mujhe lagta hai khaana - shraddha, vishwas, aansoo, pyaar, mithaas, nok jhok, yahan tak ki desh prem bhi de jaata hai. Ab tak yaad hai, 26 January ki parade ke baad, jab do motichoor ke ladoo chote se brown thailay mein milte the. Unko khane ke baad desh ke liye kuch karne ka man hota tha, aur phir poore saal intezaar rehta tha phir se 26 January ki parade ka.

Kya haseen pal the, befikri ke, Savings, future aur in sabhi khayaalon se door. Dekho, befikri ke din to "dosti" ka paryayvachi lagta hai. Meri zindagi ka ek aham hissa dost hain, shayad hum sabhi ki zindagi ka aham hissa hain dost. Toh phir... Khaane ki baat ho aur doston ka zikr na ho... aisa ho hi nahin sakta. Kahin jaana ho doston ke saath, bina khaane ke yaad hi nahin. Sabse pehle yahi sochte, "Kahan khaana hai?" Yahi batiyaate rehte. Kahin sadak ke kinare khaye hue golgappe, wo chaat-papdi ya bharma tangdi, Bahut se kisse yaad aate hain doston ke saath! Kahin cafe ki coffee, dhabay ki chai, ya phir ameer feel karne ke liye Bukhara (Delhi ka famous restaurant) ki daal makhani aur naan.

Ab kaafi deshon mein ghoom chuke hain aur bahut tarah ke cuisines kha chuke hain, phir bhi Bharatiya khaane ki baat hi alag hai. Ab tak yaad hai, kuch 20 saal pehle Europe trip mein shayad cooker bhi lekar gaye the! Kuch kaam doston ke saath hi kar paate hain. Chahe cigarette peeni aati ho ya na aaye, Hukkay ka shauk ho ya na ho, maza hi kuch alag hota hai doston ke saath, sadak ke kone mein sirf dikhave ke liye cigarette peete hue total bakwas karna. Anmol sa wo samay…yahan har baat mein koi matlab nahin hota, par har lamha yaadgaar ban jaata hai.

Aap kahan kitaab se baahar khayaalon mein gum ho rahe hain…Maana aapke dost bahut acche hain, uncle aunty bhi kuch kam nahin. Aaiye, ek aunty ka kissa sunaati hoon. Army ka bachpan raha hai mera, kyunki papa army mein the. Par jab bhi yaadon ki baat aati hai, ek aunty, jinka naam bhi nahin pata, par unke ghar khai hui Eid ki kheer ab tak yaad hai. Is had tak ki jab khana khatam ho gaya, phir bhi hum sab nai fridge khol ke chupke se khai kheer, baat hi alag thi!

Khana kyun kitna special ho jata hai, kaise koi signature dish banata hai, kaise koi apni mohar khane par lagate hai. Khana mehnat, parishram aur dedication bhi hai.Ye maine apne saas ki cooking mein bhi dekha hai.

Meri saas ke haath ka gajar ka halwa bhi kuch kam nahin. Ab tak yaad hai mujhko, ek baar unki behan, char ghante baahar chulhe par baithkar, gajar ko bhoon rahi thi. Khushboo se pata lag raha tha ki doodh ka khoya ban gaya hai, aur phir unhone bulaaya meri saas ko, ye sochkar ki meri saas tareef karengi. Meri saas aayi, dekha aur boli," Abhi to ye pakna shuru hua hai, do ghante aur lagenge." Aur phir samajh mein aaya, agar khane mein apni mohar lagaani hai, to mehnat lagti hai. Aur wahi mehnat ka nateeja hai ki aaj itne saalon baad, meri saas ke haath ka hi gajar ka halwa khate hain. Khanna kuch khaas hai.

Ek aur yaad hai unki, khaane ke saath. Jab bhi hum India se wapas aate hain, to meri saas apna pyar hamesha khane ke zariye dikhati hain. Do mahine pehle, jab Pati India sai wapse aaye the, to meri saas ne meri bitiya ke liye vishesh roop se kasaar banakar bheja. Kamaal hai, pote-poteyoon se inhein kitna pyaar hai, aur us pyaar ko darshaane ka tareeka bhi khaana hi hai. Khaana kuch khaas hai.

Kabhi-kabhi safar bhi khaane ki yaadein de jaata hai.Train mein milne wala cutlet, bus stand ki bhujia, ya highway ke dhabe ki daal tadka. Jab pehli baar Amsterdam aaye, to kahin cheese ki mehak hogi. Ab "mehak" bol rahi hoon, us samay wahan khadi bhi nahin ho sakti thi. Travel ki baat nikli, Anil ke travel ka time dhyan aa gaya. Unki naukri kuch aisi thi ki kaafi travel karna padta tha. Phir bhi, unke suitcase mein aloo bhujia na ho, aisa kabhi nahin hota tha! Anil kehte the ki "shaam ko aloo bhujia khaakar tripti ho jaati hai, jab aap ghar se door baithe hote hain." Sochiye, ek aloo bhujia tripti de! Sach mein, khaana kuch khaas hai.

Baat jab parivaar ki, rishte ki, aur khaas tareekhon ki ho, to ye kaise mumkin hai ki khane ki charcha na ho? Main Navratri ka vrat karti hoon, aur un aath dinon mein koshish karti hoon ki sirf paani, doodh, lassi ya chai par rahoon. Lekin jab Ashtami aati hai, to thoda alag tareeke se karti hoon. Kanjak bhog zaroor lagaati hoon, lekin uske baad un kanjak ki maaon ke saath baithkar Ashtami ka khaana khaati hoon, kaale chane, poori, halwa, nariyal, aloo ki sabzi aur raita, aur sab kuch bina masale ke. Aur phir chaar-paanch ghantey aise beet jate hain ki pata hi nahin chalta. Kamaal ki baat ye hai ki isse ek Anokha rishta ban jaata hai. Ye rishta na dosti hai, na koi paribhashit bandhan, lekin phir bhi, jab koi kanjak mein wo nahin hoti hain, to unki yaad bahut aati hai.

Khaane ki yahi khaasiyat hai, ye sirf pet nahin bharta, ye rishte ko bunta hai, yaadon ko sanjota hai, aur dilon ko jodta hai. Sach mein, khaana khaas hai.

Kya aankh micholi khel gaya khaana mere saath...Umeed hai aap ko mera yeh vartalap kuch aapki haseen yaadon mein le gaya hoga. Recipe to nahin keh sakti, par kuch recipe jaisa aap se share kar rahi hoon, mere liye kaafi khaas, kyunki ye recipe maa ne jaise batlaayi mujhe. Usmein yaadein sirf aankh micholi nahin kar rahi, balki un yaadon mein doobe khushi ke aansoo bhi de gayi. Ye sirf khane ki baat nahin, ye ek dil se dil tak pahunchne wali khaamosh baatcheet hai jis mein har swaad ke peeche ek kahaani hai, aur har kahani mein... maa.

Sharing my favorite food Churma's recipe which is, in English, Hindi aur yaa phir Hinglish! From the era when there were no modern gadgets, just simple cooking filled with love. Yet, the taste still brings back the same comforting feeling of ghar ka angan.

Churma – A Taste of Our Home

(From a mother to her daughter, made with love in an open kitchen on a mitti ka chulha.)

When I asked Maa this recipe for the book, Maa smiled and said "Beta, this is not just food. It is the taste of our home, of the hands that came before us, of warm mornings in the open kitchen, and the joy of cooking together. Churma is more than just a dish, it is love, patience, and the comfort of family. I will share with you how we make it, the way my mother taught me. We use to make during festive time, during travel or when the work in fields was too much, also for the ladies during pregnancy"

What You Will Need:

Flour (Aata - Wheat/Bajra Flour): We use bajra in winter to keep us warm and wheat in summer, both freshly ground at home from the grains your grandfather grew in our fields.

Milk: We heat it overnight in the wok (Khadhawni - Large Iron Wok) so it thickens and deepens in flavor.

Curd (Dahi - Yogurt): At night, we mix lassi with warm milk and let it set. In the morning, we churn it with a Biloni (Wooden Butter Churner) to make butter and buttermilk.

Ghee (Clarified Butter): The best part! Fresh, homemade, slowly churned from curd using Raee.

Jaggery (Gur - Unrefined Cane Sugar) or Raw Sugar (Shakkar): The sweetness of the earth, adding a warm, rich flavor.

How We Make It:

Kneading the Dough: Take the fresh flour (ideally in a Pittal ki Parant - Brass Bowl) and knead it into a firm, soft dough. No Chakla (Rolling Board) or Belan (Rolling Pin) here, just our hands, pressing and shaping each roti gently, just like my mother did.

Cooking the Roti: We place the Lohe ki Tawa (Iron Griddle) on the Mitti ka Chulha (Clay Stove) and let it get hot, filling the air with its earthy scent. As soon as I lift the roti with Chimta (Metal Tongs) off the Tawa (Griddle), your Mami (Aunt) sprinkles just the right amount of Gur (Jaggery) or Shakkar (Raw Sugar) over it. The heat melts it into the dough, making it soft and fragrant.

Crushing the Roti: The warm, sweet roti is broken by hand, no grinders, no machines, just the way it has always been done. We keep pressing and breaking it down until it turns into tiny, delicate grains, almost like Khoya (Milk Solids), soft and melt-in-the-mouth.

Adding the Ghee: Now comes the magic touch fresh, homemade ghee, poured generously and mixed well. The moment it touches the Churma (Sweet Crumbled Roti), everything comes together, the warmth, the aroma, the taste of home.

Letting It Rest: We cover the Churma (Sweet Crumbled Roti) with a cloth, letting the flavors settle, just like we let things in life take their time. And then,

We Serve:

The same way my Maa (Mother) made it. The same way I make it, but not anymore. Today, we have appliances. The Aata (Flour) and milk are not the same. The ghee is not homemade. The cooking range, chimney, and Mixie (Blender) have replaced the traditional ways. Churma bana aur ghar mein mehak bhee nahin. (The churma is made, but the house no longer carries its aroma.)

Reshmi Nashier

* * *

Rishton ka Swaad, Pyaar ka Zayka

Umr ke lagbhag paanch dashak mein aakar bhi maa-baap ki ankhon mein hum abhi bhi wahi pehle dashak wale bachhe reh jaate hain, iska ehsaas mujhe aksar hi hota hai, par haal hi mein ghatit is ghatna ne mere is ehsaas ko pakke vishwas mein badal diya.

Main Amsterdam se Delhi pahunchi. Papa mujhe airport lene aaye. Mere laakh mana karne par bhi woh kabhi nahi maante, "Humein toh sirf car mein baithna hota hai, waise bhi hum ghar par kuch nahi kar rahe hain." Koi na koi nai dalil unke paas tayar hoti hai. Maine kitna samjhane ki koshish ki, ki jab main duniya ke kisi aur kone se Delhi aa sakti hoon toh kya Delhi mein, jahan maine apni aadhi zindagi bitayi hai airport se ghar nahi aa sakti hoon? Khair in sab baton ka koi fayda nahi, kyunki aaj tak main airport se ghar kabhi bhi akele nahi gayi hoon. Aksar main raat ko Delhi pahuchti thi par is baar main subah mein pahuchi. Car abhi thodi door hi chali thi aur main sabka haal-chaal pooch rahi thi, itne mein papa ne kahha, "Itni lambi flight se aayi ho, bhook lagi hogi, lo kuch kha lo." Unhone apni mutthi kholi aur us mein tissue mein lapete hue do *thekua* they. Main papa ki oar dekhi aur ek tak dekhti hi reh gayi. Mere aankhon se paani aise nikla jaise koi baandh toot gaya ho. Kitni shakti hai khane ki cheez mein. Khana sirf hamare sharir ko urja pradan karne ka sadhan nahi, balki yeh hamari bhavnatmak jeevan ka ek mahatvapurn hissa hai. Mujhe yeh ehsaas hua ki yeh hamari purani yaadon ko taza aur rishte ko majboot rakhne ka ek atoot zariya hai.

Mujhe abhi tak yaad hai ki hum sab bhai-behen poora din apne college aur office mein vyast rehte, par raat ka khana sab saath milkar hi khate they. Papa ko thandi roti khana sweekar tha par sab koi saath na khaye bilkul bhi pasand nahi. Woh ek jadui samay hota tha. Sab ke paas kuch na kuch kehne sunne ko hota. Woh pal khushi aur masti se bharpoor hote they. Is samay ka mahatva kewal bhojan ke swaad mein nahi balki us sneha mein tha jo har niwale ke saath mehsoos hota. Khana toh bahut hi saral, sadharan aur shakahari hota. Wahi dal, roti, sabzi kyunki meat aur machli toh hum aksar saptah ke ant mein hi khate the. Par woh ek saath bitaye hue samay ka mahatva kuch aur hi tha.

Bihari parampara ke anusaar Shanivar ko khichdi aur bhartha ka nishchit menu hua karta tha par jis din ka sabko intezaar rehta woh tha Ravivar. Subah ki kiran jab khidki se ghar mein pravesh karti tab se rasoi mein halchal shuru ho jati. Subah ke nashtey mein poori aur aloo ki rase wali sabzi. Uska swaad abhi tak zubaan se nahi utarta. Nashtey ke baad papa market jakar mutton laate. Din ke khane mein chawal, arhar ki dal ke saath mutton curry aur aloo bhujia ka hona anivarya tha. Har baar mutton laane jaane se pehle maa ka papa ko yeh kehna ki "fresh hoga tabhi lijiyega" bhi utna hi zaroori tha.

Rasoi ghar maa ki jaagir thi aur papa us se koson door rehte, lekin ek cheez thi jo sirf papa hi banate, aur woh thi caramel custard. Unki college ke dino ki yadein jo judi thi us se! Bade hi shauq se papa hamesha apne kisse kahaniyan sunate hue anda aur doodh phent te aur phir cheeni se caramelise ki hui katori mein yeh mishran daal kar cooker mein steam karte. Jab bhi caramel custard ka naam sunti hoon toh papa ke banaye hue is dish ki yaad aati hai.

Shaadi se pehle maine kabhi akele khana banane ki zimmedari nahi uthayi. Shaadi ke baad jab khana banana shuru kiya tab sabziyon ko bhi achhe se pehchan na nahi aata tha. Ek din raat ko khane par maine dekha ki mere pati dev bade shauq se roti ke saath sabzi kha rahe the. Mujhse woh sabzi khaye na jaaye. Maine thodi der baad pooch hi liya "Kaisi bani hai yeh sabzi"? Unhone bade chaav se khate hue jawab diya "bahut hi badhiya". Maine mann hi mann me socha ki Bhagwan mujhe aisi sabzi agar roz khani padi toh main khana nahi kha paungi. Mujhe rona sa aa gaya aur maa ke haath ke khane ki badi yaad aayi. Baad mein pata chala ki maine lettuce ko cabbage samajh kar banaya tha. Woh shaadi ka pehla mahina tha, isliye shayad pati dev ne kuch nahi kaha ya unhe ehsaas tha ki sabzi chahe bani kaisi bhi ho, woh kis bhavna aur dular ke saath banayi aur khilaayi gayi thi. Khana banana aur parosna apne prem aur sneha ko vyakt karne ka ek uttam madhyam hai. Us kadvi sabzi ne humare rishtey ko mithas se bhar diya.

Kehte hain ki avashyakta hi avishkar ki janani hai aur yahi achhe khane ki chaah ne mere khana banane ke safar ki shuruat ki. Shuruat mein toh maine kitabon par hi bharosa kar naye naye vyanjan banaye. Jaise ki prayogshala mein hota hai kuch safal hue aur kuch nahi. Shuruat mein kafi asafaltaey hath lagne par bhi maine dhairya banaye rakha. Jab kuch nahi bhi accha banta toh bhi usse bahut kuch sikhne ko milta. Khana khane ke shauq ne mujhe kabhi mayoos nahi hone diya. Shuruat mein toh maine aksar bharatiya khana hi banaya, kabhi sambar toh kabhi kadhi, kabhi dhokla toh kabhi fish chop. Naye shahron aur naye deshon mein rehne ke karan mujhe vibhinn desh ke khane ka awasar mila. Dheere dheere jab dusre deshon aur kshetron ke dost baney, toh maine un deshon ke bhi paramparik vyanjan seekhe. Khana sirf pet bharne ka sadhan nahi balki desh videsh ki sanskriti aur unki paramparaon ko logon se jodne ka uttam madhyam bhi hai. Iske liye ek vyapak drishtikon ki bhavna aur sabse avashyak hai nai cheezain sekhne ki ichha. Maine desh videsh ke khane se, jo mujhe achha aur swadisht laga use apne rojmara ke khanpan me apnaya. Yahan tak ki kuch videshi vyanjan ko mere bachhe indian hi samajhte the. Iska ehsaas mujhe tab hua jab meri beti ne bataya ki bachpan mein woh mere banaye hue tiramisu ko bhartiya mithai samajhti thi. Baad mein bade hokar use pata chala ki woh toh Italy se aaya hai.

Meetha ka toh mujhe bachpan se hi shauq tha. Aksar janamdin wagairah par main cake banaya karti thi. Shaadi ke baad jab Caribbean mein rehne ke liye pahunchi toh pastry aur ice cream ke toh bahut dukane thi par bhartiya mithai ki ek bhi nahi. Shuruat mein toh cake, pastry khane mein bada maza aaya par jab tyohar aaye toh us samay bhartiya mithaiyon aur ghar ki badi yaad aayi. Har tyohar par maa tarah tarah ke vyanjan banati thi. Chahe Holi ho ya Diwali, ghar par gulab jamun aur dahi bade zaroor bante the. Isi liye shayad humare ghar bhi aaj tak har parv ya tyohar ya koi bhi utsava ya samaroh per iska hona jaroori hota hai. Teej ka toh kya hi kehna, us din pura parivar ek saath milkar *pedakiya* banata. Aksar raat ko khana peena khatam hone ke baad yeh karyakram shuru hota. Hansi mazak aur kisse kahaniyon ke beech sau se bhi adhik *pedakiya* dekhte hi dekhte ban jaate. Yeh tyohar sirf pooja paath ke liye nahi balki banaye hue khaas pakwan aur mithaiyon ke swaad se humein bachpan ki yaadon se jode rakhte hain.

Desh-videsh mein tarah tarah ke vyanjan banane ke bawajood mera pehla pyaar mithai hi hai, usi ki chahat ne mujhe khana banana sikhaya. Aaj main bade shauq se tarah tarah ki mithai banati hoon. Bade anand ka ehsaas hota hai unke banane par. Meetha se yaad aaya ice cream ka, jisne humare parivar ko ek majboot bandhan mein bandha aur dilon ko jodne ka sadhan bana. Meri sagai ka samaroh tha. Karyakram khatam hone ke baad sirf ghar ke kuch log reh gaye the. Arranged marriage hone ki wajah se hum sab ek doosre ko utne acchi tarah se jaante bhi nahi the. Tabhi mere hone wale pati ne khaa, chalo ice cream khane chalte hain. Aur kya tha mere bhai-behen ke chehre par muskan aa gayi. Hum sab Nirulas pahunch gaye. Wahan par sab apni pasandida swaad ke baare mein batein karte karte ek doosre ko jaan ne lag gaye. Us khushnuma mahaul ney ek ajnabi ko jeeju bana diya. Jeeju ke saath hansi mazak aur masti ka mahaul bana. Us ice cream ne rishtey ki gaanth ko bhavnatmak roop se hamesha ke liye jod diya.

Jaise ice cream ne ek naya rishta jod diya, waise hi mere banaye hue vibhinn pakwanon ne anya rishte gehre kiye. Duniya ke zyada tar sanskritiyon mein har khushi ki pehli abhivyakti bhojan hi hai, isliye tyohar, janmadin, vivah ya khushi ke kisi bhi avsar par khana, dawat ya party ka hona jaroori hota hai. Isi liye main khana banana seekhne ki yatra mein aage badhti gayi. Samay ke saath saath yeh meri kushalta aur atmavishwas ko aur bhi badhaati gayi. Kaal chakra kuch aisa chala ki ab main toh khana banati hi hoon, par ab mere bachhe bhi mere saath milkar khana banate hain. Ghar par koi vishesh dawat ya tyohar ho toh unka saath hamesha hota hai. Shayad woh bhi apni zindagi ki yaadein jod rahe hain ya apne aapko us kala se jod rahe hain jo ki na sirf unhe atmnirbhar banati hai, balki dosron ke liye pyaar aur dekhbhal dikhane ka ek amoolya madhyam hai. Khana sirf khana nahi hota apno se pyaar jatane ka bahana bhi hota hai.

Kahani toh shuru hui thi thekua se, par akhir yeh thekua hai kya?

Thekua Bihar ka ek paramparik nashta hai jo gehun ke aate, ghee aur gud se banaya jata hai. Chhath pooja ke dauran thekua Bhagwan ko chadhaya jaane wala ek pojaniya prashad hai. Purani paramparik sanskriti ke anusaar koi mehman kisi ke ghar aane par thekua le kar atey they. Yeh aksar subah ya shaam ke chai ke saath khaya jaata hai. Meri bachpan ki yadein isse judi hai aur meetha hone ke kaaran mujhe behad pasand bhi hai.

Thekua banane ka samaan.

Gehun ka atta-2 cup

Gur-¾ cup

Nariyal ki gari-3-4 chamach

Elaichi powder-1 chamach

Saunf- 1 chamach

Ghee-moyan aur talne ke liye

Thekua banane ki vidhi.

Ek bade se parat me gehun ka atta le kar, usme shudh ghee dal, ache se use milaye. Itna ghee dale ki jab hathon se atte ke ladoo banaye toh woh bandh jaye. Agar ladoo bandh raha hai toh isme moyan theek hai.

Sahi santulan hi har cheez ka saar hai.

Ab is atte me Saunf, chote chote kate hue sukhe nariyal ki gari aur gur (jisko pani ke saath ghol bana ke rakha hai) milaye. Pani dalte hue halke hathon se ek sakht atta goondhe.

Jeevan me bhi aur rasoi me bhi, har cheez ka ek yogdan hota hai.

Ab iske chote ya bade apne pasand ke loi banaye. Phir har loi ko thekua ke sanche per dabakar sunder thekua banaye. Is tarah sare loi ko sanche per dabate hue sunder thekua bana le.

Hunar aur mehnat se har cheez nikhar jaati hai.

Ab dheemi aanch per ek karahi me ghee garam kare. Jab ghee achhe se garam ho jaye toh usme jitne thekue aa sake dal de. Inhe charo taraf se ulat palat kar halke bhure rang ke hone tak tal le.

Sabr ka phal meetha hota hai.

Inhe nikal kar kisi channi per rakhe taki atirikt ghee nikal jaye. Isi tarah saare thekua ko tal le.

Swad ka raaz, apni reeti riwazon mein chhupa hota hai.

Satya Akhouri

✳ ✳ ✳

Musings

मंथन

OF A SILENT AWAKENING AND UNTOLD MEMORIES

The many moments etched deep down, un spoken and silenced over the years. Moments that refuse to fade away and struggles to stay alive. That stained dress hidden under the bed, a startled gasp, a father's cautious reassurance—yet nothing could erase the confusion of an innocent mind as the body transformed to adulthood. So very natural yet shrouded in secrecy and left unexplained.

The mockery of a child struggling to express in a language unknown and the attire which was ripped off by unwanted gaze. The desire to be a few shades lighter merely to be accepted as a woman as the rest of her never really mattered. A father's aversion to weighing his daughters in dowry and the daughter's realization that as a mother she played out her role in all sincerity as simply those were the times.

The doubts the fears the standing alone the faith and the loss of faith- the musing untold written down at last

ME AND MY RANDOM WORDS

MY FIRST BLEED

S must have been around eleven years and a few months, not yet twelve. She had been noticing something strange for the past few days. It was not clear to her what was happening, but it was something unusual. No matter what she did, she could not get rid of the slight staining on parts of her clothes. Unable to comprehend and not sure who to ask, she kept hiding her undergarments under the bed, very sure they would never be discovered. If she was not feeling unwell, whatever this mysterious ailment was could probably be kept under wraps. Unfortunately, that was not to be. While collecting the laundry Sunday morning, Mummy discovered the pile under the bed and gave out a squeal, followed by her usual "Oh my God!".

It was impossible for S to deny, and she blabbered out, 'I think I am ill.'

Mummy started laughing and called out for Bapi. 'I don't know how to even explain all this.' She sounded kind of surprised and at the same time a little unsure.

Yes, 'S' was me, and I had no idea what Mummy had to explain. Neither could I understand why she was laughing when it was evident something serious had happened to me.

Bapi came up, took me by the hand, and sat me down on his knees. Tears were rolling down from my eyes, as it was clear to me the illness was serious. Bapi calmed me down in a way only he could and then explained that it was no illness – the stains were proof that I had reached puberty. Completely flabbergasted, I listened to him as he explained in the simplest of terms what was menstruation and how, from here on, it was going to be a monthly affair.

It all sounded strange and confusing. I tried to make sense of this new thing called 'periods'. I kept wondering how come I knew nothing about it; nobody ever told me this was to be expected. I was feeling a little foolish and wondering if the ignorance was entirely mine. In the midst of memorizing tables, history dates, keeping up with endless school assignments, lessons on morality, choosing right from wrong, how come 'periods' never came up?

A matter so complex and so alien for my eleven-year-old self that I spent days in physical discomfort as my mind tried to make sense of it all. It meant I could have a baby when I grew up (that is what Bapi had said). But how exactly? Was it to be like the gifts I asked Santa to bring every Christmas that mysteriously appeared in my stockings every December 25th morning because I had been a good girl?

There is a reason why it's always in plural. This is, of course, a theory I conjoined over the years: The word 'period' is much more of a finality, an end of some sort, whereas 'periods', the plural, justifies the repetitive nature of the event and also somehow represents the end to a child's innocence – in some ways, the beginning of being a woman or the final act for a girl to qualify as a woman in the world. I feel the word is rather odd since it is so much more than merely something periodic.

Years later, in high school, I understood the science of reproduction and the role of menstruation in the cycle of birth, but paradoxically, societal norms kept sex elusive and shrouded in secrecy from a teenager. I was left to grapple in the dark and imagine the unimaginable – often confused and scared even with the most innocent contacts with a male.

Many years later, as an adult, when it all unfolded, I realized there was so much more to my periods than merely qualifying me to bear a child. Why was the enjoyment, excitement, pleasure, and thrill of SEX kept unknown? If only I had known better, the pain of growing up could have eased. The fear, the stress, the right and the wrong touches could have been avoided, and the first period pains, thereafter the monthly recurring discomfort, of an eleven-year-old could make some sense after all. If only sex, the inevitable, was explained and not maligned as a vice.

My God

I prefer the word 'Almighty' to 'God'. Somewhat, it makes more sense. Given the etymology of the word 'God', it kind of makes it a little biased to certain religions. But then that's the thing I was never clear about: the exact connection between religion and God (aka Almighty). Does one really need both, given they are distinctly separate? Is it not that we can reach the Almighty without the religion, and, vice versa, be a religious fanatic without being remotely close to the Almighty?

Then there are Godmen and women, a group I disdained from a very young age. I maintained a safe distance from this group of humans who claimed to be a direct connect towards reaching the Almighty and to know exactly how we mere mortals had to conduct ourselves. Growing up in India, I had seen many of them. There was a transactional relation with the blind believer, one of hypnosis, magic, and fakery, but what amazed me most was how the cerebral lot were easily seduced and gave in unquestioningly. I could never comprehend how come their faith in their Almighty was so feeble. Why were they so unsure of their own prayers and felt the need for a mortal being to reach HIM?

There is the Almighty why, then, do I see a father retrieving a decapitated body of an infant from under the rubbles of a building? Why do I see a malnourished mother holding on to a frail newborn as it suckles from a long-dried breast? Why does a teenager get raped? Why does the perpetrator enjoy luxury while an honest man of colour rots in jail? Why does She have to sell herself every night to put food on the plate while there is enough to feed all five times over? Why, for some, does hard work never pay while some have it just too easy? Why is justice so often delayed? Why is equality not really a thing? Why does she have a stunning face and mine is so scarred?

The Almighty is supposed to judge me by my work, my deeds. Why, then, do I need to fast and feast, why do I need to cover and bare, why do I adorn black or white, why do I need to burn incense and candles to appease HIM and have my voice heard?

My relationship with the Almighty has always been a complicated one. Each time I have been dealt an unfair blow, I questioned him, I was angry at him, and I doubted his very being. In the midst of insufferable pain and injustice, I fail to see his presence.

I ask myself, do I believe in his presence? I honestly do not know, but I know when I fall, I need to look up and see that HE is there. But I cannot feel him in a sculpture, in a framed picture or within the cacophony of a closed space or even in the silence of a bejewelled edifice.

My Words

Words are a strange thing – they have a way of coming back to you. I often feel they get lodged in a deep interior of the brain, in a sedated stage, and from time to time, something provokes them to come alive. They are never really gone; they are always there.

Probably that's why someone (can't remember who it was) in my childhood told me to be mindful of the words I throw out into the universe, for it seems they can never be taken back or erased out.

It happened decades ago, when I was a university student in Europe. Most of my friends were white, from different European countries – not by choice, but by circumstance. I never befriended people based on race or nationality. If anything, I sought diversity, preferring to engage with students from different backgrounds rather than confining myself to the Indian group.

Oleg was Russian white, brilliant, a few years senior to me, and a close friend. That day, as we rushed between classes, I pulled him aside in the corridor, asking if he could help an Indian girl struggling with campus housing. He knew most of the officials and was always eager to assist – whether out of genuine concern or to satisfy his ego, I never quite knew.

I had introduced him to Neelima before, but when he failed to recall, I described her: tall, slim, long black hair. There were only two other Indian girls on campus besides me. With a casual shrug, Oleg remarked, "It's so difficult you all Indians look so similar, I can't distinguish one from the other."

I was perplexed. It was absurd. Neelima and I couldn't have been more different – I was short, plump, wore glasses, had cropped hair; she was tall, slender, fair-skinned, with long braids. Yet, to him, we were indistinguishable.

At the time, I brushed it off. But as the years passed, those words stayed with me, echoing in unexpected moments. What I once dismissed as an offhand remark, I later recognized for what it was: steeped in racism, condescension, and perhaps even sexism.

I have no idea where Oleg is today, but his words endure, tarnishing a friendship that once mattered. For a woman of colour, it was one of the most blatant racist remarks I had to endure.

That's the strange power of words. They don't fade; they linger and reshape memories.

Highly myopic, I wore glasses from the age of three, and each year, they got a little thicker as the power kept progressing. Girls those days were constantly encouraged to be mindful of their looks, and spectacles were surely not considered to enhance one's looks in any way. Being almost bat blind without my glasses, I had resigned to the fact that I would always have the ugly frames perched on the ridge of my nose. Myopia was not curable. Not that the glasses bothered me a great deal, but at times, I felt it was a hindrance to looking good, especially in my early teens, when a girl suddenly becomes more conscious of her outward appearance. One day, in the presence of my grandfather, a rather distant relative casually commented, 'You have beautiful eyes. Why don't you switch to contact lenses?' Without a second's hesitation, my grandpa said, 'Indeed, she has such beautiful eyes that they need to be showcased in glass.'

Never since that day did, I feel uncomfortable wearing my glasses. They gave me immense confidence and became an inseparable part of my being. I loved wearing my glasses, and even when there was a possibility to switch to lenses and show off my apparently beautiful hazel eyes, I preferred to keep them in a glass showcase.

Words have a way about them. At times, it's better unsaid.

It was my first trip home, to Delhi after I got married. Before marriage, as soon as I would land in Delhi, which was an annual affair since my student days, I would rush home to my parents' house. But this time, it was different; I was going to my husband's parents' place – my in-laws' house, not my home. It was not my choice but a societal norm which I had agreed to abide by. Anyhow, after spending a few days at my in-laws', I casually remarked that I would be leaving for home to spend some days with my parents. Someone remarked rather candidly, 'This is your home now. You are going to your mother's house for a visit.'

In the Indian society, a girl's home is supposedly her husband's house. The remark was not wrong, but for me, at that moment, home meant so much more, and those remarks came across as somewhat unsettling. The only home to me in Delhi was my parents' house; it could be no other. That single remark snapped a bond before it was made. It alienated me from a relationship which I was just in the process of developing. If only she had not tried to replace my home with another, things would have been so different in the years to follow, and maybe I would have made a new home too.

Words have a way. They have the power to make and to break. As I chronicle these moments, I shudder to think how many times I may have been casual and careless with my use of words. Unintended, silly, meaningless words that should not have been thrown out there. Words once set free can never be called back or erased.

Shayonti Chatterji

❋ ❋ ❋

Peeling the Onion

Did you know that each layer of an onion takes its own time to grow? As the vegetable matures, some layers dry up and fall off. Just like how the onion seed transforms into a full onion, every new layer is added over time.

As the layers fell, they moulded a village girl....

Speaking Myself into Silence

Raw out of a village in Haryana, a child stepped into Kendriya Vidyalaya. I was barely aware of the world beyond my own rustic upbringing, rooted into the village culture. I spoke Haryanvi, a dialect embedded in my roots. The English language was way beyond my grasp, as was the polished urban Hindi. I distinctly remember that day in school. The teacher asked me to fetch the key for a lock. I walked up to her and confidently, in all my innocence, said, "Taley kii taali dena." The class erupted in laughter. I stood, frozen, staring back, unable to comprehend where I had faltered. It seemed the most apt question: she wanted me to open a lock, and I asked for the key. That day, in that very moment, unconsciously, I throttled the carefree soul within, the voice which never feared to express or speak out. As if a layer of my being was unpeeled forever. Today, in a different time and space, I often wonder how speaking out in my mother tongue could be a cause for ridicule and humiliation. For a child, it was not the most obvious. Why were my words dampened in laughter?

Life unconsciously shapes us through its experiences, leaving behind permanent imprints, never to be erased. That's why today, when someone remarks that I don't speak Haryanvi like a true Haryanvi despite being a Jaat, "Dil mein ek thahaka uthta hai, kuch vyang ki tees ke saath"(a wry chuckle rises within me, one laced with both irony and an unspoken sting). Wasn't it ironic, I ask, that the school carried a Hindi name, yet within its walls the pride lay in speaking English? While my confidence to express myself was brutally unpeeled, I took upon questioning society's double standards and its ridiculous norms entrenched in hypocrisy.

CAMOUFLAGE 101: MY JOURNEY TO BECOMING UNNOTICABLE

Growing up in India, I learnt that to stand out was almost inviting trouble and attracting the wrath of society. Boys had a right to freedom that we girls could never claim. They were at liberty to devour girls with their eyes, track every move without so much as shuffling a foot. Their mere gaze was enough to assassinate and peel off all dignity. I sometimes felt like saying, "Ghar thuk chhod ke aaoge aankhon se?". I recall once seeing a friend humiliated, her long skirt lifted in front of a hundred silent observers. No one spoke that day; no one came up to help. She burst into tears, went home, and never wore a skirt again. That day, another layer was cruelly unpeeled, and I took over the mantle of safety. Those were the times when throwing acid on a girl's face was disturbingly common, simply because she was deemed too beautiful, or she had the audacity to say no. The growing realization set in: it was safer not to stand out; it was better to carry oneself in a way that made you almost invisible. And yet, people today struggle to understand why dressing and freedom are intertwined.

I have adorned a shroud of invisibility ever since. Yet when the skirt was lifted, a thought crossed my mind: The day when I can decide for myself what to wear and actually wear it, that would be my true independence. A layer of hope and independence began to form alongside. I was convinced if someone dared to pull my skirt up, I would definitely stand up for myself. It sounded rebellious at the time.

In one instance, when I was in my late twenties, at my brother's wedding, someone was teasing – first my sisters (which I wasn't aware of) and then tried the same with me. My immediate reaction was to turn around, face up to the culprit, and then, with the maximum force I could muster, I left an imprint of my hand on his cheeks. It was as if I was venting years of pent-up anger. Life always wraps us up in two layers: one that we cannot avoid, derived directly from life's numerous experiences, and the other, a subtle and beautiful inner layer that unfolds within the unconscious mind. Life brings along its moments; some remain, while others fade away. These moments shaped me as a person and the personality I reflect to the world today.

Another amusing incident of my life: On a bus, an elderly woman reminisced about a time when girls married at twelve or thirteen. 'You stay attractive for the most part of your marriage,' she explained. "Those days, there was no makeup to hide your flaws, so it was better that way." For a second, it made sense. Then my heart ached. If beauty was to be the foundation of marriage, then love truly was immaterial, a simple nonsensical figment of the imagination. Yet another layer, the acceptance that outer beauty dictates one's worth, engulfed me. The concept and necessity to stay desirable to be valued unconsciously cemented in my mind.

A relative had just given birth to a baby boy. Someone asked, 'What's his complexion?' The reply: 'Ladke ki ek hi cheez theek honi chahiye, baaki sab chalega.' Laughter followed, but it wasn't sarcasm; it was pride. Gender differentiation was not just accepted; it was celebrated. In my childhood, fairness creams only targeted girls, reinforcing the notion that beauty was their only currency. At a very young age, I learned my society made gender bias completely normal, accepted, and a matter to be celebrated.

No Manual, Just Blood

The day I had my first period, the sarcastic barbs and my ignorance made me feel so very vulnerable. It all unfolded in a rather innocent way, a day etched in my mind forever. I remember I was at the hospital to treat a knee injury; the wound was bleeding profusely. When the nurse bandaged my knee, I casually mentioned that there seemed to be a lot of bleeding even on my thighs, which she needed to check. Everyone in the room, nurses, patients, cleaner, burst out laughing at the little girl and mocked, 'Your dress is blood-stained at the back. Maybe you should go home.' Jis pal maine kamre mein kadam rakha, unke chehron par ek dabi hui hansi thi, jo turant thahake mein badal gayi.

The label of ignorance was slapped on me by medical personnel. Was that not ironic? Perhaps, a shame that only I could feel. I felt frustrated because instead of offering to help, they just advised me to go home. We were raised to not question our elders; it was almost programmed into us. Respect meant silence, even when something felt wrong. So I, like many others, quietly went back home. This collective silence, this ingrained habit of not challenging authority, grew from a culture where violations were often normalized. "Bade hain, samajh jao," they said. And so we did. We stayed silent. We swallowed discomfort. We walked away instead of speaking up. Because in our world, questioning adults was disrespectful. Challenging authority was rebellion.

But what happens when that authority crosses the line? When an uncle's touch lingers too long and is dismissed as affection? When a stranger's elbow digs into your ribs in a crowded auto, and you're told to adjust? These weren't isolated incidents, they were part of a culture that taught us to endure instead of resist. Violations were normalized. Boundaries blurred. And we were expected to stay quiet, smile politely, and carry on. We weren't just conditioned to stay silent, we were trained to believe that our silence was maturity.

Beneath all the layers of superficial conditioning, I am still me -Reshmi. Independent, fun-loving, courageous, sensitive, and outspoken. Sometimes I pause and wonder, how? How did I remain whole despite being an unwilling witness, or at times a victim, to many harsh realities: extreme punishments, verbal and non-verbal abuse?

PEARLS FROM PAIN: LESSONS THAT SHAPED MY SHINE

Ironically, the same society that imposed silence and shame also gave me my faith, in kindness, in resilience, and in God. The same hands that hurt, were also capable of healing. The same voices that silenced could also soothe. A paradox of experiences shaped me, some sharp enough to wound, others gentle enough to heal.

Sometimes life offers its biggest lessons in the smallest, most unexpected moments. I want to take this opportunity to share one such moment with my father, a short interaction that quietly shaped how I approach mistakes and uncertainty. I was driving a car for the first time with my dad beside me when, while parking, I accidentally hit a cyclist. From the driver's seat, it looked terrifying, as if both the person and the cycle had gone under the bonnet. My hands froze, and before I could react, my dad calmly said, "Reshu, don't move the car even a millimetre." I asked what to do, and instead of panic or blame, he gently said, "Let's get out and see what needs to be done. Accidents can happen." That softness, without losing firmness, gave me the courage I needed. To our relief, the cyclist and the bicycle were both completely unharmed. Still, my dad insisted we take him for a check-up, just to be sure. When I asked who would drive now, he simply said, "Reshu beta, you will." He didn't give me a lecture or a lesson, but his calm presence and unwavering trust showed me that mistakes may happen. What defines us is what we choose to do next. In that quiet moment, he planted in me a strange but lasting confidence to face whatever life may unfold. Another layer of discomfort was peeled in a strange, unexpected event.

As far as I remember, my mother had her own burdens to carry, brought upon by the world she lived in. She married at eighteen, couldn't pursue studies, but ensured that her children would stand on their own feet. I pursued engineering, not because it was my true calling, but because in 1900s in India, it felt like there were only two respectable options, doctor or engineer. Maybe then I didn't understand it quite well. But today, at fifty, I see the truth. I understand that my mom tried her best to raise me without her own layers. There was full honesty and sincerity at her end. Her experiences shaped her, just as mine shaped me.

Like her, I, with Anil, mera pyara half, also tried with sincerity and honesty to shed these acquired, enforced layers. And I know I have done my best to ensure that my children grow without them. Perhaps one day, they will write their own stories, their own truths, without the weight of unnecessary layers binding them.

Sometimes, life feels like that jar where onions and garlic are shaken, their peels falling away with each shake. And lately, I've come to feel that maybe life is shaking me too, not to break me, but to help me let go of what I no longer need. The masks I wore, the fears I carried, the versions of me I thought I had to be. One layer at a time, they fall away.

The strength to face it all hasn't come from some grand moment, it's come from countless small ones. Like that soft voice of my father saying, "Accidents happen." Like the quiet steadiness of my mother, who once gave up her own dreams, saying, *"Main padai puri nahin kar payi par meri beti zaroor padhegi."* That one decision lit the path I now walk. Like a prayer whispered during chaos. Like a moment of silence that felt like guidance. These moments, big and small, have built something unshakable in me.

My faith

In God,

In life's deeper wisdom.

And in the lines that have anchored me for years 'Hum panchi unmukt gagan ke, pinjar bandh na gaa paayenge' (a poem by Shivmangal Singh Suman), I was reminded that I was never meant to live in a cage. None of us were. The soul was meant to move, to sing, to breathe freely.

I am not perfect. I make mistakes. But I learn, sometimes slowly, sometimes painfully. And with every shake life gives me, I'm starting to believe… Maybe all of this is shaping me into something more honest, more whole.

Maybe, just maybe, all these peelings are making me a pearl.

Yes, Reshmi is a pearl, just as we all are, shaped by the sediments of experiences.

Har raat ka apna ek gehra sa raaz hota hai,
Aur har khamoshi ke peechhe ek dua chhupi hoti hai.

Zindagi sawal zaroor poochhti hai,

Magar har jawab shor mein nahi milta.

Kabhi kabhi, sirf ek vishwas ka saaya kaafi hota hai

jeene ke liye, muskurane ke liye, aur moti ban jaane ke liye

Reshmi Nashier

✳ ✳ ✳

❋ ❋ ❋

And now we come to the final story of this book. Jab sawal dil se uthte hai toh maa ki godh me suni aur sikhi hue bhasha hi yaad aati hai. It is for this reason that this piece has been originally written in hindi but transliterated in roman script so that it can be shared with all of you.

Shayad ye lekh aapke kuch sawalon ka jawab de sake, ya phir aapko apne aap se kuch sawal karne ke liye prerit kare.

❋ ❋ ❋

Zindagi ka Asli Romance

Kya Hum Kabhi Samajh Payenge...?

Zindagi ek prem kahani ki tarah hoti hai, jahan sirf chahne se kuch nahi hota, na hi sirf mehnat se, aur na sirf aastha rakhne se. Kuch kahaniyan tab hi mukammal hoti hain jab chahat, mehnat aur vishwas, teeno ek hi dhadkan mein simat jate hain. Lekin kya hum kabhi samajh payenge ki ye sab kis kram mein aur kyon hota hai? Kyon kuch cheezein humare niyantran mein hote hue bhi nahi hoti?

Hum kitni baar kisi cheez ko puri shiddat se chahte hain, uske liye din-raat mehnat karte hain, aur fir bhi vah humein nahi milti? Fir kisi aur samay, jab hum utni bhi koshish nahi kar rahe hote, wahi cheez achanak humare samne aa jati hai. Yeh kyon hota hai? Kya sach mein sab kuch humare niyantran mein hai, ya koi aur shakti humare liye raste tay kar rahi hai? Agar sab kuch tay hi hai, toh fir hum mehnat kyun karein? Agar mehnat hi sab kuch hai, toh fir kuch cheezein kyon kabhi nahi milti, chahe hum kitna bhi prayas kar lein?

Humare jeevan ki asli shakti ka raaz kya hai? Kya yeh hamari kathin mehnat, hamara atoot vishwas, hamari aastha, ya fir in sabhi ka anmol sangam hai?

Mere Hero... Mere Papa

Hum apne jeevan ke moolya aksar apne mata pita ya apne bachpan ke anubhav se seekhte hain.

Mere pita ki chaar betiyon mein se main sabse badi hoon. Ek aise samaj ka hissa, jahan betiyon ko chinta aur bojh ki tarah dekha jata hai. Unhe ek jimedari samjhi jati hai. Aksar bachpan me jab bhi rishtedar milte, toh unki ankhon mein karuna aur afsos jhalakta, aur munh se anayash hi ek thandi saans nikalti, "chaar-chaar betiyan!"

Lekin mere papa bilkul alag hain. Wo zindagi ko khul kar jeene mein vishwas karte hain. Accha khana, ghumna-phirna, latest fashion ke kapde pehnna, unki fitrat mein hain. Aur yeh sab wo sirf apne liye nahi, balki doston aur rishtedaron ko bhi wo tarah-tarah ke tohfe dena aur badhiya bhojan karana pasand karte hain.

Sabse aham baat, unhone kabhi betiyon ko chinta ki tarah nahi dekha. Humein kabhi yeh mehsoos nahi karaya gaya ki hum ladkiyan hain toh kisi cheez mein kam hain. Humari shiksha par poora dhyan diya gaya, humein achche schoolon mein bheja gaya, aur humein kisi sanche mein daalne ki koshish nahi ki gayi. Khana banana, kadhai-bunai karna shaukiya tha, na ki anivarya. Humein kabhi kamzor nahi, balki saksham maan kar pala gaya.

Kai baar doosre mata-pita ko hamesha apni betiyon ke ird gird ghoomte dekh, unhein kabhi akele nahi chhodte dekhkar mann mein yah vichar bhi aata ki kya unke mata-pita un se zyada pyaar karte hain? Ab main piche mudkar dekhti hoon toh yeh ehsaas hota hai ki woh swatantrata, atma-nirbharta aur atmavishwas ki pratham seedhi thi.

Maa se aksar rishtedar aur dost apni betiyon ke dahej ke liye ikattha kiye hue paise aur sone ke zevar ke baare mein baatein karte. Unhein paise kam kharch karne ki naseehat bhi dete.

Maa papa ko daraane ki poori koshish ki jaati. "Chaar chaar betiyan hain, inki shaadi ka intezam kaise hoga?" Maa bhavishya ko lekar aksar sahm aur dar jaati, par papa sirf muskura dete.

Ek baar maa ne pucha hi liya ki kya zevar denge hum apni betiyon ke dahej mein, toh papa ka jawab tha, "unke report card." Unke liye betiyon ki shiksha hi sabse bada khazana tha.

Papa ne apni chaaron betiyon ko kabhi chunauti nahi, balki apne jeevan ka sabse anmol hissa maana. Unhone kabhi samaj ki parwah nahi ki. Uske banaye hue niyam nahi maane, balki apne khud ke niyam banaye.

Aaj main aur meri behnein sab apni shadi shuda zindagi mein safal aur khush hai aur apne apne kshetra mein aage badh rahe hai. Par yeh sab kaise mumkin hua? Kya yeh sirf mere papa ki kathin mehnat thi, jo unhone apni betiyon ke liye ki? Ya phir unki apni aastha thi, ki agar sab kuch sachche dil se chaha jaye, toh zindagi apni raah dikhati hai ya yeh betiyon ka naseeb tha?

Sanwle Rang Ki Kahani

27 saal ki umar mein jab videsh mein ek anjaan sales lady ne mujhse kahaa, "Your skin color is so beautiful!" to main dung reh gayi. Mujhe vishwas

hi nahi hua ki usne sach kaha hai. Mujhe laga ki woh apna samaan bechne ke liye meri jhoothi badaai kar rahi hai. Par jhoothi hi sahi, maine zindagi mein pehli baar apne rang ke baare mein kuch accha suna tha. Pehli baar kisi ne mere us pehlu ki prashansa ki thi jisko lekar mujhe apne desh mein hamesha kum samjha gaya.

Bachpan mein jab mausam se beparwah khel-kood kar ghar aati toh aksar maa kehti ki achhe se sabun laga kar nahana taaki saaf lago. Mujhe bachpan mein lagta tha ki saaf lagna matlab dhool-mitti dhona hota hai. Par jaise-jaise badi hui, har padosi, rishtedaar, yahan tak ki raah mein chalte anjaan vyakti ke paas bhi hamesha rang saaf karne ke nuskhe hote. Koi kehta haldi besan lagao toh koi kaccha doodh. Koi aisa gharelu nuskha nahi bacha tha jo mere upar nahi azmaya gaya. Lagta tha jaise main ek samasya hoon, jise sab milkar suljhana chahte the. Har roz ek naye tarah ka uptan tayaar milta. Tarah Tarah ke vigyapan ladkiyon ko gora banane ke liye radio aur tv per sunai aur dikhai dete. "Gorepan ka raaz", "jaldi gora bane", yeh sab sun-sun kar main apne hi rang se anjaan si ho gayi thi. Kya tha akhir ki sabko bus gora banna tha?

Mujhe yah samajh mein nahi aata tha ki jab main sanwle rang ki hoon toh mujhe gora banane ki koshish kyon ki ja rahi thi. Kya gora rang hi khubsurti ka ekmatra maapdand hai? Kya sirf gore rang wale hi sundar hote hain, kya sanwla rang sundar nahi hai? Yeh sawal mann mein umarte rahe, par jawab koi nahi de pata. Samaj ki aankhon mein ek hi rang chaya hua tha aur woh tha gora rang.

Hamesha aisa laga jaise rang meri kabiliyat se zyada mayne rakhta hai. Chahe woh shaadi ke rishte ke samay ki baat ho ya school mein nritya natak ki mukhya bhumika. Shaadi ke rishton mein pehli nazar rang par padti, gunnon par nahi. Ek baar kisi aunty ne kaha tha, "Ladki achhi hai, par rang thoda daba hua hai." Us pal aisa laga jaise main ek vastu hoon, jise sirf dekh kar taula jaa raha tha.

Videsh mein jaakar yah ehsaas hua ki jo rang Bharat mein meri kamzori thi, wahi rang yahan ke logon ko sundar lag raha tha. Tab yah mehsoos hua ki sundarta ka koi ek paimana nahi hota balki yeh ek samaj ki banayi hui dharna hai. Hum sab bhinn bhinn rang ke hain aur sab logon mein ek alag sundarta hai. Iska ehsaas hote-hote lagbhag ek chauthai zindagi beet gayi aur woh bhi ehsaas pardes mein kisi paraye ne karaya.

Badlav tabhi sambhav ho paata hai jab hum andar se uske liye tayyar hote hain. Ek videshi ke shabd ne ek chingari lagai, lekin aag toh mere andar pehle se hi lagi hui thi. Mujhe ye bharosa tha ki agar main khud ko sweekar karungi, toh duniya bhi mujhe apnayegi. Yeh atm swikriti mere chahne se aayi. Maine ise paane ke liye khud per mehnat ki. Lekin kya yeh badlav mere chahne bhar matr se hua? Ya kya yeh pehle se hi tay tha ki meri soch ek din badal jayegi?

Kumbh Mein Aastha Ki Dubki

Saal 2019 mein Kumbh mele me jaane ki tivr ichha hui, lekin laakh koshishon ke bawajood jaana sambhav nahi hua. Mann ko samjha liya ki shayad sahi samay nahi tha. Lekin jab 6 saal baad Mahakumbh ka samay aaya, toh aisa laga jaise koi adrishya shakti mere liye raste bana rahi thi. Main wahan pahunchi, Ganga mein dubki lagayi, aur vah ehsaas shabdon se pare tha, jaise kisi bacche ko uski maa ne apni godh mein samet liya ho.

Kya yeh mahaj sanyog tha ki tab nahi, lekin ab main wahan thi?

Kumbh ka anubhav sirf ek dharmik yatra nahi thi, balki yeh mere vishwas ki pariksha bhi thi. Kya hum sahi maayne mein bharosa rakhte hain ki jab cheezein hamare paksh mein nahi hoti, tab bhi unka koi gehra arth hota hai? Kya hum samajh sakte hain ki kuch cheezein hamari iccha aur mehnat se nahi, balki brahmand ke sahi samay se judi hoti hain?

Jab Prem Poora Hota Hai…

Zindagi sachmuch ek prem kahani ki tarah hai, yahan sirf ek tarfa chahat se kuch nahi badalta. Use paane ke liye mehnat bhi karni padti hai, aur jab kisi mod par raah dhundhli lage, toh aastha ki lau bhi jalaye rakhni hoti hai. Pyar ki tarah, yeh bhi tabhi falta-foolta hai jab chahat, mehnat aur vishwas teeno milkar ek saath dhadakte hain.

Jab hum apne sapnon ko poore dil se chahte hain, unke liye parishram karte hain, aur yeh vishwas rakhte hain ki sahi samay aane par cheezein humare paksh mein hongi, tab zindagi hume wahi lauta deti hai jo humne usme dala hota hai. Jeevan ki har cheez ko poori tarah samajhne ki zarurat nahi balki use mehsoos aur apnane ki zarurat hai. Is bharose ke saath ki jo bhi ho raha hai wah kisi na kisi kaaran se ho raha hai, chahe woh kaaran humein abhi samajh mein aaye ya nahi.

Shayad yahi zindagi ka asli romance hai....

Satya Akhouri

❋ ❋ ❋

Did Our Stories speak to you ?

If our moments have awakened a memory, a thought, or a feeling you've long meant to put into words—why not start now? Every story deserves to be told, and perhaps this is the first page of yours. After all, stories live on when they are shared. Maybe yours is waiting to be written.

We'd love to hear from you! Whether you want to share your own experiences, tell us what this book meant to you, or simply connect, drop us a message at **connectwithpuchka@gmail.com**

❋ ❋ ❋

The Moments I Seized And the Ones That Got Away

Growing Older: A Gift, A Challenge, A Journey

Food: My Greatest Joy... Or Is It?

Stories Still Waiting to Be Told

Here on,
It's all about You...

9 798899 069932